Yangchow Years

by
Grace Harvey

Yangchow Years
First Edition
Published by DreamStar Books, September 2003

Lasyard House
Underhill Street
Bridgnorth
Shropshire
WV16 4BB
Tel: 00 1746 761298
e-mail: dreamstar@jakarna.co.uk

Set in 'Garamond'

Copyright © Grace Harvey

The moral right of Grace Harvey to be identified as author of this work has been asserted by her in accordance with the Copyright, Designs and Patents Act 1988.

All rights reserved. No part of this publication may be reproduced, stored in a retrieval system or otherwise, except brief extracts for the purpose of review, without the prior permission of the publisher and the copyright owner.

Printed and bound in Great Britain by Antony Rowe Ltd

ACKNOWLEDGEMENTS

The following people have all contributed information and recollections for this book:

Joan and Myfanwy Beynon
David Bolton
Eleanor and Phyllis Box (from Lunghua, *not* Yangchow C)
Rosalie Duckitt
Peter Gibson
Walford Gillison
Brenda Henderson
Jean Irvine
Marjorie Lee
Patsy Longhurst
Cyril Mack
Ian MacKinnon
Mary Lou Newman
Gilbert and Owen Manley
June Martin
Albert and Mona Nissim
Colin Palmer
Carol Parry
Mary and Denis Savage
Beryl Smith
Heather Sulerzyski, daughter of G. D. Grant
Peter Wickings

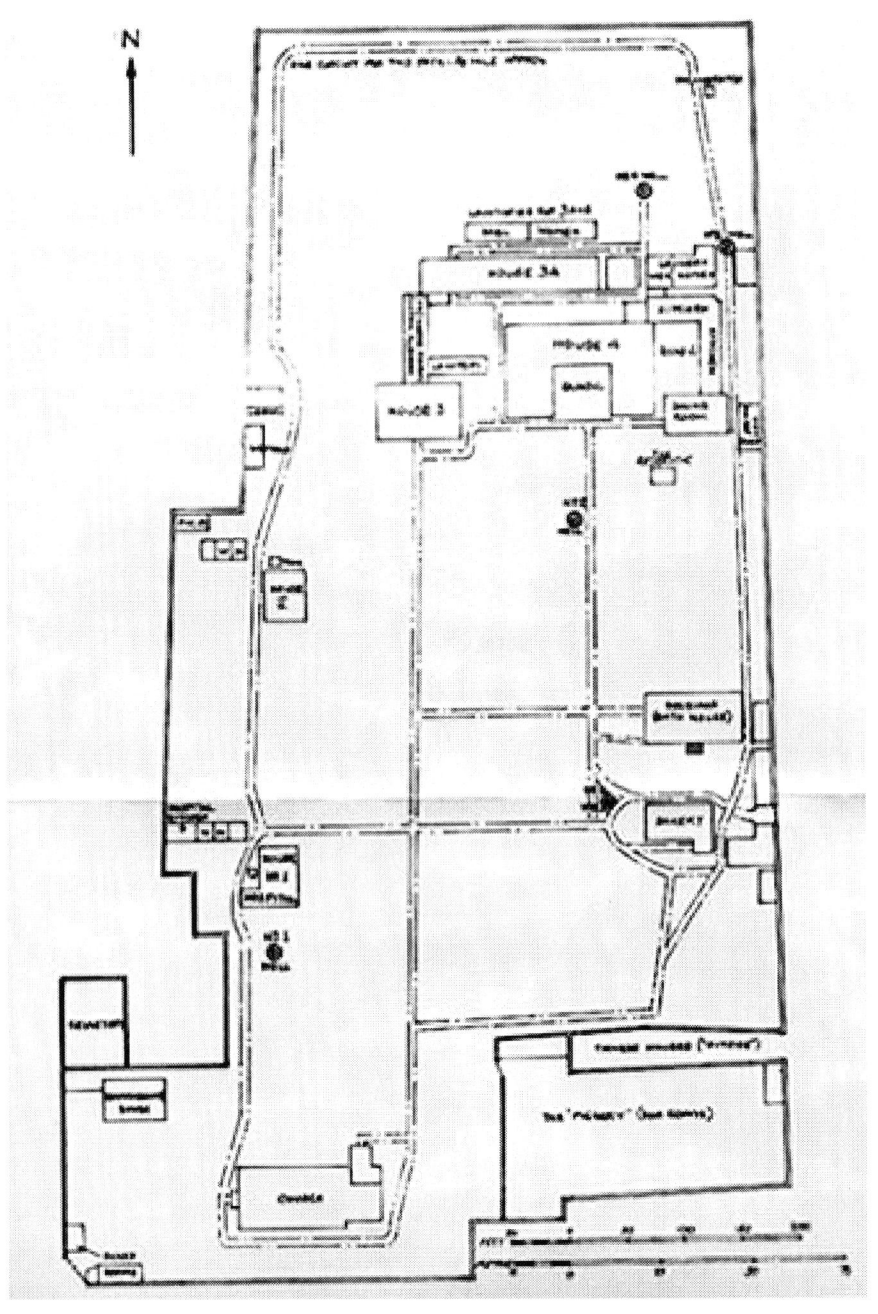

Yangchow Camp C plan

CONTENTS

		Page
1.	Introduction	1
2.	Harold and Mary	2
3.	Leaving Shanghai	12
4.	Arrival	15
5.	Food Glorious Food	24
6.	Water	35
7.	Clothing	41
8.	Footwear	48
9.	Billeting	51
10.	The Compound	61
	Photographs & Drawings	68
11.	Births, Marriage, Death	80
12.	Fatigues	84
13.	People	96
14.	Health	106
15.	Schooling	118
16.	Religion	134
17.	Parcels	147
18.	Isolation	154
19.	Japanese	163
20.	Administration	181
21.	Entertainment	186
22.	Festivities	201
23.	Sports and Pastimes	203
24.	The End	209
25.	Appendix I: Camp Residents	213
26.	Appendix II: Bibliography	220

PREFACE

This book tells the story of two and a half years' internment, during which I and my family were imprisoned by the Japanese authorities at Yangchow C Civil Assembly Centre. Yangchow, an ancient walled city, is situated 160 miles north of Shanghai, on the Grand Canal. We were there from March 1943 to early October 1945, with some six hundred other British, Canadian and Americans. My parents were missionaries, but most of the other people came from the flourishing business community of Shanghai. We learned of the war ending rather late; after the arrival of Allied troops to relieve the camp, we left Yangchow for Shanghai, en route for home.

INTRODUCTION

"Horrid! I won't eat it!" said small Mei-mei.
"You must", insisted Dad.

The child pouted and kicked the legs of the stool she sat on. She knew her father would soon have to go out, to teach his VIth form History class. Stubborn resistance took hold of her. She had only to sit it out. Her father would go; then the enamel bowl of unappetising rice and vegetable stew would be removed by her mother.

The time? Midday, in summer, partway through our time in Yangchow internment camp, towards the end of World War II. The place? Our home, a small cubicle divided from the other families in the church, by partitions of straw matting. The church was part of an American Mission compound, now Yangchow camp C, under Japanese authority. The child? A six-year old, with round face, and brown eyes. Within the family circle, her name was Mei-mei – Chinese for 'little sister'. Gradually, though, people were starting to call her 'Grace'. Me.

The obstinacy of six won that particular battle. Mei-mei knew her mother was softer than her father, who could be stern. She played on this difference, though she could not yet express the thought in adult fashion. Why did her father insist? Two reasons: children should be obedient. Also, food was short, very short, and none should be wasted, even if it was the same old stew.

HAROLD AND MARY

How was it that Harold and Mary Wickings, my parents, came to be in China at all? They married in Leeds after a long engagement, on July 30th 1930; there were to be two children of the marriage, Peter, my elder brother, born in March 1936, and me, Mary Grace, born some 20 months after, in November 1937. My father had offered his services to the London Missionary Society, of Livingstone House, at Westminster. The Society appointed both parents to the Chinese mission-field. Initially they were to learn Mandarin Chinese at language school in Peking in 1930/31.

Both parents were from Northumberland, my father from Newcastle-upon-Tyne, where his father worked for Armstrong's, the great ship-building firm. On first leaving Rutherford College, his secondary school, Dad went into the Armstrong drawing-office, as a draughtsman, just as his elder sister had done. So he helped to design many of the fighting ships of World War I. The names of all the vessels in each class of destroyer were so familiar to him that he expected his children, Peter and me, to know them, too. He was immensely surprised when we could not chant "And there's Renown, and Repulse, and …" After the war ended, his decision to enter the Congregational ministry, meant four happy, if penurious years, at Edinburgh University, studying for his M.A. degree. Theological training at Yorkshire United College, Bradford, followed. Here he learnt New Testament Greek, and Biblical theology, as he sat at the feet of Professor C. J. Cadoux. From Cadoux, Harold absorbed a lifelong enthusiasm for the Bible, especially the New Testament. Ever afterwards, he was a scholar manqué. In Yorkshire he grew to respect the warm-hearted, if brusquely spoken, people, of Bradford and Wakefield. He also made friends – among them, Arnold Mee, who became a pastor in Keld, Swaledale, and John Marsh, whose career led him to Oxford, as Professor, and Principal of Mansfield College.

Meantime Harold had fallen in love with Mary Thorp, my mother. She was the younger of two daughters of the manse; her father, Rev. William Thorp was Presbyterian minister at Chatton, miles away from Newcastle, near the Cheviot hills. William Thorp was a widower; Mary, his daughter, kept house for him. Not till his death was she free to marry and, with her husband, embark upon the great adventure of China.

In personality they were a contrast: my father articulate, with an impish sense of humour, energetic in manner, able to make the party go, when he was not reading or writing in his study. He was a superb preacher, not afraid to use the dramatic gesture to enforce his points, or to vary his voice in pace or tone, if he deemed it appropriate. My mother was shy in company, never one to startle others with vivacious talk. But her gentle goodness impressed all who knew her, whether they were the Chatton folk who adored "Miss Mary", or later on, L.M.S. colleagues, and the Chinese people who came to love her. It is never easy to describe goodness, but her serenity shone through.

The atmosphere of their retirement home in Kent impressed Sarah, my daughter, as a small girl. "It's so lovely at Granny's house" she would say, through her tears, as we left.

Mother's face, seen at its best in profile, was beautiful when she was in her twenties and thirties. Once an intrusive landlady in Yorkshire asked my father why he had no photograph of his "young lady" for her to dust, as she tidied his dressing-table. This was when they were engaged, or rather, in the old-fashioned phrase, "had an understanding".

> "I can see my girl on every hoarding" Dad proudly replied. "She's the image of the girl in the Palmolive soap advert ... !"

Back to Peking in 1930 ... The newlyweds savoured their time there, making the usual expeditions to the Great Wall, and the Ming tombs, and learning to adjust to the harsh winters. My father taught my mother to ride a bicycle, as they skated through the dense Peking traffic, under the noses of the camels, used for transporting every kind of load – rice – cabbages – silks – through the streets. It was a carefree time.

Then my parents moved south to Central China. They soon had a mission-station of their own, at Siaokan, where an elderly couple, the Gellers, were about to retire. Siaokan, a walled town, like Yangchow, had a leper hospital as well as the L.M.S. premises – a church and accommodation for the missionary family, and the nursing staff attached to the hospital.

Peter Ross, my brother, was born in 1936 in the Union Hospital, Hankow. His birth as a boy and the firstborn, was greeted with fire-crackers. By now my parents were due for furlough in England, so they travelled home by P&O liner to introduce their baby son to his grandparents, and to his two adoring aunts. I was born when they lived in a furlough house in Selly Oak, Birmingham; no fire-crackers for me. But Dad would tease me, on each birthday, on the brass plate outside the door:

"You'll be famous, Mei-Mei"

When I asked what the words on the brass plate were, he took the wind from my sails, by telling me they gave the name of the nursing-home in Moseley, Birmingham, were I was born.

In May 1938, my father returned to China alone, leaving Mary with us two little children. It was hard for my parents to be separated. Later in life they were reluctant to be parted from one another. We all met up again in Shanghai in 1940. My father met us on the quay. The story goes that I ran up to him, clasping him around the knees, as I exclaimed:

"You're my dear Daddy!"

He swung me up into his arms, and then Peter, too, for a hug. We travelled up the Yangtse in December 1940 with a halt at Hankow for my parents' missionary friends to greet Mary and the children. I learnt to

Yangchow Years

chant my alphabet in a sampan – a Chinese fishing boat, half covered with reed matting – under instruction from my brother and father.

Our Siaokan home was a fine house, with green shutters, and a verandah, which had a swing, made specially as a gift for Peter. As in most Western households in China, there were servants: a cook, an amah, and a gardener, who served the entire L.M.S. community, including the English hospital staff, who were unofficial aunts to Peter and me. The garden seemed vast and beautiful to our young eyes. Both parents delighted in its trees and shrubs, its honeysuckle, which they called "gold and silver flower", translating the Chinese name for us. Shwenny, the son of the Chinese gardener, was our only playmate. All three of us were fascinated by aeroplanes, so we fabricated our own from spare bits of wood, begged from the carpenter. Peter was pilot, Shwenny gloried in the oil-can as engineer; as a mere girl I was air-hostess, my uniform a thin cotton playsuit, with a shoulder strap always halfway down one arm. My only girl friends were imaginary; they had girlie names, like 'Rosebud' and 'Violet'. One of them lived by the green wooden rainwater butt. I was heartbroken when we had to leave Siaokan, and I had to bid these friends goodbye. Worst of all, I had to leave my new dolls' pram behind, too. The Japanese took over our house, and all its possessions. I sobbed as I thought of some small Japanese girl playing with that dolls' pram.

Arriving in Hankow under Japanese guard in April 1942, we were confined to the Union Hospital grounds until we departed for Shanghai in August of the same year. The few months at Hankow were a difficult, confused period for all L.M.S. missionaries, considering the Japanese threat to mission property, and possibly, to their lives. Could anyone leave for England; if so, who should go, and who stay, as a nucleus for both the church, and for Chinese patients of the hospital? Some wives were keen to return; others were affronted at the very suggestion. What would happen to the Chinese Christians? Could their church life survive? All these points were discussed, and prayed over, by the Box family, the Gillisons and our parents, and by other colleagues, as they were to be discussed later in Shanghai.

A Japanese sentry guarded the entrance to our mission compound. There was a complex system of permits for anyone leaving, whether to shop, or, if one of the medical staff, for consultation with other doctors in Hankow. The sentry demanded a rake-off on everything purchased, as his right. So the Chinese messengers would drop their goods over the compound wall, before they met the sentry's acquisitive gaze. [1]

Meantime Peter and I had other English children of our own age to play with: Walford Gillison was a year or so older than Peter, Phyllis and Eleanor Box some years older again. We were happy enough in the fine compound garden, so full of flowers, and only restive when the teeming summer rain forced us to be indoors. The adults feared a recurrence of the terrible flooding so frequent in Hankow. Our parents spent their free time in the evenings with impromptu concerts, or listening to gramophone music. Someone organised a tennis tournament, and my father bemoaned his lack of social skills to the pages of his journal. He was far more appreciative of the play-reading of Ibsen's *A Doll's House* which he thought very good. All the time, he and the others were saying goodbye to some of their Chinese friends; Chuffey – the nickname of one of his Siaokan close friends - was off to West China. Just then Dad was expecting to return to England, so he commented:

"Sad to leave China. When shall I return?" [2]

Leaving Hankow

Following Japanese orders, our party of mission-folk left Hankow for Shanghai in mid-August 1942, travelling by river. The river steamer, Hsing Yiin, had a Swiss flag painted on the boat deck, as protection. Our family was fortunate to be together in a good 2nd class cabin, unlike some others relegated to 3rd class quarters. The Japanese carried out a thorough inspection of all inoculation certificates, on two occasions during the four-day journey. Nanking my father thought was a melancholy spot, with memories of the Japanese excesses when they captured it at the start of the Sino-Japanese war in 1937. We journeyed downstream past Chinkiang till the vessel anchored off Woosung point at evening. With his eye always out for shipping, my father found it strange to see so few fishing boats on the Yangtse, almost no familiar Chinese junks, just a few Japanese steamers. A Swiss consular representative greeted us on arrival; then all were taken by bus to the Columbia Country Club just outside Shanghai. Here families were split up:

> "Mary and the bairns upstairs with others."

The men were to sleep in camp beds in the bar; my father's companions were Stuart Craig, Martin Shepherd and Jowett Murray, all L.M.S. colleagues.[3]

"Bairns" is the Scottish term for children. Both parents were staunchly Northumbrian. It was the place where they had met, and courted; so Peter and I, all our young life, heard tales of Bamburgh on its black rock, of Hadrian's Wall, of my father's first bike ride from Newcastle to Otterburn and back, all of sixty miles. All we knew of England was filtered through a Northumbrian haze: the tragedy of Flodden field, the battle of Otterburn and the bitter fighting between the Percy and the Douglas, the birds of the Farne Islands, the heroism of Grace Darling, the ballad of the Laidly Worm. All these tales we heard as we sat perched on Dad's knee. He could speak the broadest Northumbrian, and would chant:

> "Round the ragged rocks, the ragged rascal ran"

– then inciting us to copy the Northumbrian initial 'R' – so far back in the throat. Of course, both Peter and I failed miserably. "Hinny-bairn" – the equivalent of honey-chile – was a favourite endearment. Along with this saturation into Border lore, went a distrust of the Stuart kings – so by the time I was five, I had learned of untrustworthy Mary Queen of Scots, of Charles I, her grandson, and later of both Charles II and James II. So, however great the romantic appeal of the Cavaliers, I could never be anything but a Parliamentarian, even as young as 6. I had imbibed support for Parliament almost with my mother's milk. My mother was strong on nursery rhymes, chanted and sung. She brought us up to revel in Lewis Carroll, and *The Water Babies*; best of all, she sang, so that hot summer nights in camp when I could not sleep were soothed by her singing, as she waved a sandalwood fan to cool me down.

Dad loved reading aloud to us; there was always a bedtime story. Usually it ended on a cliff-hanger: would Ratty and Mole find the young otter, in *Wind in the Willows*? All the Pooh and Piglet stories of A. A. Milne, *Heidi*, some Arthur Ransome, Louisa Alcott. We began with *Little Men* – probably for Peter's sake. My father was an inveterate reader himself – whether of theology, of books on the archaeology of Hadrian's Wall, of Conrad and A. J. Cronin, or of biographies like George Seaver's life of Edward Wilson of the Antarctic. Both of us caught the disease of reading from him, as he first taught Peter his letters and numbers at Siaokan. To my parents' surprise, I learnt to read almost without knowing it. Dad's amazement when I could read to him from my book of *Snow White* shines from the page of his diary. Then he would tease me over the names of the dwarves, making up soubriquets like 'Dumpy' and 'Spotty', to accompany 'Bashful' and 'Dopey'.

Columbia Country Club

From August 1942, we lived with many other British people at the Columbia Country Club, in western Shanghai. This had begun life as an American sports club; now it became home to us and some 300 other Westerners, till internment proper began in March 1943. This was our first experience of living at close quarters with others, since the C.C.C. was intended to sleep 35 people. Families were split up, so that mothers and children shared the large bedrooms upstairs; single ladies slept in the corridors. My father slept in the former bar, other men in the erstwhile bowling alley – all on camp beds. Men were not supposed to go upstairs at all. This could be a problem, as Dr. Kenneth McAll discovered, when his wife, Frances, had to go into hospital. Young Elizabeth, their daughter, was just over a year old.

> "It was certainly impossible for Ken to have Elizabeth with him in the bowling alley. He often had to attend to her needs after the other family in the room had gone to bed, so had to feel his way in the dark. He then had to determine whether or not she needed changing. She invariably did and it is not an easy matter even for a more experienced mother to change a nappy by feel only ..."

Meals were eaten in the communal dining-room, first of all in the disused swimming-bath; later when the weather turned chillier, we ate in the former billiard-room. Everyone at C.C.C. had to come to terms with those who snored and with those whose nights were marked by bad dreams. About half of those at C.C.C. were missionaries, from all the societies: Baptists (B.M.S.), Methodists (M.M.S.), L.M.S. like ourselves, China Inland Mission, S.P.G. and C.M.S., too. There were enough missionaries for a football team to play the non-missionaries; the score was drawn 2-2. [4]

Being at the C.C.C. was not a bad time, though all the adults hated the loss of privacy. We children now had plenty of others to play with; my parents would take us together with other L.M.S. children: David and Ruth Murray, and Alison Craig, to Jessfield Park for picnics, or just to run about among the coloured leaves of autumn, catching them as they drifted down. Peter and I both went to school, at first to a private school. In January 1943 Peter was old enough to join the transition class at Shanghai's Cathedral School.

All enemy aliens were required by the Japanese to wear red armbands; American were marked 'A' while British people had a 'B' on theirs; each initial was followed by a serial number. Apart from this, there was little restriction on our movements in Shanghai. My father was concerned to further the book he was writing: a harmony of the four gospels; he was eager to get it in shape for publication, so would borrow a bike, and dash off to the printer's. Just before Christmas, his diary runs:

> "My one concern: to show Jesus to the common man." [5]

This "harmony" was a major preoccupation for Harold in the months before internment. His dealings with the Shanghai printer, his eagerness to view specimen pages recur throughout the entries for February and March 1943. He corrected proofs late into the night, and was overjoyed when he could compile a synopsis. Tom Allen, a B.M.S. friend, soon to enter Pootung, helped Harold check the index. The problems of translating the harmony into Mandarin were discussed with a Chinese friend. Harold felt he left it in safe hands, before we left Shanghai. Two copies of the harmony arrived in one of the parcels which reached us in Yangchow. Harold was critical of the binding, but wrote, with pride:

> "The first copy must go to Mary." [6]

The Japanese questioned my father one November afternoon about his finances and property at the Club:

> "I have no property! Made out list of furniture etc. abandoned at Siaokan – but really no point in giving the list: there won't be any compensation."

After the war was over, my father with his L.M.S. colleague, Stuart Craig, returned to an overwhelming welcome at Siaokan, from both Christians and non-Christians alike. All the Chinese were eager for the hospital to be re-opened. The buildings had not suffered too much, but Dad's boxes, left in the leper hospital there, had been looted. He wrote to Fay Westwood:

> "I had left my best books, certificates, important papers and my camera ... Alas! Everything has gone. I must not moan when so many people have lost homes and loved ones, but I had scraped ever since my student days to build up those treasures; some were college prizes. Never mind." [7]

At this time, in 1943, my parents' relationship was under threat from the intrusion of a third person. Usually they were close to each other.

Mother was acutely aware of how much she depended on unmarried friends in caring for us children. In Hankow, and now in Shanghai, my father felt one particular friend was too close to Mother. We could never leave Columbia Country Club – whether to shop, or to visit Jessfield Park for a picnic, as a family of four – without the company of this lady, making five. Dad was hurt by this relationship; he felt excluded by it. The problem solved itself, with internment in 1943. The lady in question was in another camp, not with us in Yangchow. My parent's relationship reverted to its usual even keel of affection and support. After the war, both Mary and Harold rejoiced, when their friend made a happy marriage.

---

[1] Gillison, *The Cross and the Dragon*, p.156. Also HFW, diary for 1943, passim
[2] HFW, 25 May 1942
[3] HFW, 18 August 1942
[4] Frances McAll, *The Moon Looks Down*, pp.30-2; HFW diary, passim
[5] HFW, 21 December 1942
[6] HFW, February/March 1943 passim and 9 June 1944
[7] Letter quoted in Angus, p.171

LEAVING SHANGHAI

The British in Shanghai learned of their impending internment in February 1943. People had to get rid of many possessions: the Piper family sent tennis racquets, gramophones, bicycles and typewriters for auction, before the Japanese could seize them. Joan Main records the Japanese eager confiscation of cameras, radios and binoculars. But when each family knew which camp it was to enter, they invested in camp chairs, folding stools, and as many tinned foods as they could afford. Our family, too, bought enamel mugs and plates; Dad painted our distinctive surname on them, together with our camp numbers, too. Saddest of all preparations, family pets had to go. The day before the Pipers departed, Beryl wrote:

> "This morning took Bill, our dog, to be put to sleep ... Poor old Bill." [1]

More than a week of packing preceded the departure of the Piper family. Beryl was confirmed: there were no white dresses, but the girls wore white veils pinned on in the vestry before the ceremony. On two separate days, Beryl visited the dentist: a sensible precaution. The family beds were despatched, along with bedding, tableware, buckets and six huge candles. A Chinese friend brought his parting gift of tea, sugar and coffee. They were pleased to learn that some acquaintances, Colin Palmer, Valerie Judah and Leslie Popple among them, were to share their internment in Yangchow. The tragic news of Jo Farrin's suicide in Shanghai's dreaded Bridge House prison reached Beryl, who noted it along with the destruction of 105 Japanese 'planes in an air battle off New Zealand. [2]

From the time all British nationals were ordered to report to Shanghai's Anglican Cathedral, the Japanese authorities strove to put the best possible face on internment:

> "The Civil Assembly Centre being the best home for those who live in it, must be loved and cherished by all of them. Each person shall take care of his health and live in harmony with each other. There shall be no disputing, quarrelling, disturbing or any other improper misdemeanours." [3]

The guards in the Civil Assembly Centres – the Japanese euphemism for internment camps – were Consular Police – not fighting men of the Japanese army. Many were actually Koreans, press-ganged by the Japanese into serving their ambitions in east Asia. There were copious instructions: we were to bring beds and bedding, mosquito nets and four items of luggage each; clothing, tableware and sports equipment were listed too. The instructions sounded a puritan note when they advised married couples against bringing double beds – presumably on grounds of limited space, both on the journey, and when they arrived.

> "The things mentioned … must be simple and unostentatious, strong and durable." [4]

Most people packed folding chairs and tables, together with their tableware and any tinned food they had, into their bundles of bedding. How impressed Fay Westwood and her mother were, when they saw one family arrive at the Cathedral grounds; all their luggage was carried by two strapping teenage sons who bore long bamboo poles

> "laden with suitcase after suitcase and hamper after hamper, all swinging loosely by their handles. They even carried a gramophone …" [5]

People glanced nervously about, venturing a smile when they recognised friends, wondering about those unknown to them. After a roll-call, we were marched out of the Cathedral gates, down Kiukiang Rd., on to the Bund. People moved

> "in a sort of loose orderly formation. There was some light banter and joking … but really we did not know one another well enough to relax and communicate freely."

As we walked Chinese onlookers lined the streets. Keith and June Martin recognised their German doctor who came down to wave goodbye to them. Then we boarded the launches, which took us to the steamer. [6]

---

[1] Joan Main, unpublished memoir, p.14. Beryl Piper, 1-9 February, and 12 March 1943
[2] Beryl Piper, 1-9 March 1943
[3] Instructions from Japanese Consul to British and American nationals, quoted in Cliff, p.30
[4] Instructions from the Japanese Consul General, February 1943
[5] Joan Main, unpublished memoir, p.16 and Angus, p.104
[6] Cyril Mack, recollections, October 2002, and Keith Martin, recollections, May 2003

ARRIVAL

The Yangtse and the Grand Canal

> "We are now prisoners! Oh – no different from before in many ways"

exclaimed my father to his diary, as we travelled up the broad Yangtse river, and the Grand Canal, to Yangchow. Our steamer was the "Hsing-Yiin Maru", the very same in which we had journeyed from Wuhan in August 1942. We children were in a cabin, with our mothers, while Dad slept in the common room, with others, in the stern of the vessel. [1]

The Mack family – Cyril and Roy with their parents – were in the same group. All four had a space below deck, on the tatami – Japanese sleeping-mats. A Japanese gendarme checked family names and entrance numbers against his list. Unfortunately for Cyril and Roy the water-pipe above their accommodation sprang a leak, soaking their tatami. It took some re-organisation to make the family even tolerably comfortable for the overnight journey. However all four of them had not been separated from one another; this was a great consolation. [2]

Chingkiang, some 150 miles north of Shanghai, was the place on the south bank of the Yangtse, where we were transferred to barges, for the journey up the Grand Canal. Fay Westwood, with her mother and aunt counted themselves lucky in being near the end of one of these barges, as they had slightly more breathing space than others, and could see clearly ahead, on their journey north. But it was impossible for most people to sit on the five-hour trip, though they could sit on their luggage, taking turn and turn about with other people. Sanitation was completely lacking: all very well if you were a man, as you could relieve yourself over the barge-rail. Not so easy for women and children:

> "Someone emptied a small tin can of its precious contents. A circle formed facing out – with backs to the can and its occupant. Each time the can was used, the waste was emptied into the canal. It was the beginning of indignity."

Young Fay was desperately embarrassed, and further mortified when her mother took her turn to use the can. This was the first, but by no means the only time when sanitation was to be of enormous significance:

> "Class distinction paled … we had merged into a tired, apprehensive conglomerate of people, levelled by the demands of the basic functions of the human body." [3]

But for Cyril Mack, the journey on the canal was a revelation. He had always lived in the city; this was the first time, apart from a brief expedition with the Wolf Cubs, that he had seen the Chinese countryside: peasants working in the rice fields, oxen yoked together:

> "The vast countryside, the other barges passing on the canal, some with sails up, and some being poled – the friendly chat between the bargees as they passed – it was so different, unexpected and colourful.."

Disembarking, when we arrived at the grey city walls of Yangchow, was not easy. The Japanese guards, armed with swords, were in a hurry. Hence everyone had to walk the plank, that is, to go along the first of two planks some twelve inches wide, and twelve feet long. One end of the first plank was on the barge containing the Mack family; the other end rested on a stationary barge, beached partway between their barge and the stony bank. A second plank, similarly narrow, led directly to the bank. It took some courage to cross the two plank bridges, with luggage, since the water below was deep, and also because of the bounce and whip which the planks developed, threatening to throw off those who had to cross these temporary bridges.

Nonetheless, young Cyril was fascinated by Yangchow harbour:

> "The steep banks on either side of the Grand Canal were crowded with humanity. Barges were loading and unloading, children were swimming, there was a babble of voices and cries ... And looking down on this ... panorama was the massive grey ancient city wall."

The wall was wide enough for two vehicles, travelling in opposite directions, to pass one another, on top of the wall, as we were soon to see from the compound where we were imprisoned. [4]

When the last group, including Brenda Smith and her family, arrived, some of the party were taken off to B camp at a small jetty, before most of them continued on in the boats to the harbour proper. This was on 19th March 1943. [5]

Whenever we arrived, all of us had to walk through the narrow streets of Yangchow city till we reached the American Episcopal Mission School compound – Yangchow Civil Assembly Centre – Camp C. It, too, was bounded by a stone wall, nine feet high. We entered through wooden gates, thick and solid.

> "As we approached the gates the full import of our situation would have hit us and we filed through quietly." [6]

As soon as we entered the compound, Commandant Yamashita gave a long harangue, translated by Mr. Grant, our Camp Representative, for our benefit.

> "We were told the Japanese had brought us here to protect us, and that now it was our 'happy home'."

We were advised not to try and leave; the guards had orders to shoot to kill anyone attempting escape. The commandant made clear that each adult would have to perform duties essential to the camp's smooth running. Yamashita's order that we were to think Yangchow our happy home had long-term implications for Jean Willis, wife to Chris Willis, of the evangelical Brethren. After liberation in 1945, Jean only left Yangchow with great reluctance, despite her longing to see her children in Canada. [7]

The old city of Yangchow was long established as a regional capital and administrative centre. It is situated on the Grand Canal, some 160 miles north of Shanghai. The Canal itself was constructed to link Peking, the capital, to the rich rice-growing parts of China. In the 1940's Yangchow was still a walled city, like our medieval cities of York and Chester. To this day a few old streets remain among the shining modernities of the new China. Tradition has it that Marco Polo, the Venetian traveller, was the city's governor, in the late thirteenth century. Kublai Khan trusted the young foreigner to govern this area, of which Yangchow was the centre. The evidence? It comes from Marco Polo's own account of his travels. Possibly he exaggerated his importance; maybe he was only a minor official in the Imperial civil service. Some Chinese scholars disagree; they explain the lack of Chinese evidence about Polo's authority by the destruction of many records of Kublai Khan's dynasty. Since Kublai had recently acquired southern China, the territory of the Song dynasty, he needed administrators for his new acquisitions. The Song officials were not trustworthy, and Mongols, Kublai's own race, were few in number. So Kublai use the "coloured eyes" – the Chinese name for foreigners.

Yangchow had local fame as the regional capital for the collection of the salt-tax, in old Imperial China. Salt was an Imperial monopoly; the salt-tax will have operated in China much as the gabelle did in France, prior to the 1789 Revolution.

Yangchow Years

The story in Yangchow is that Marco Polo arrived to take up his three-year stint as governor, at the city's east gate. The gate has now vanished, along with the last of the city wall, in the 1950's. But East Gate Road still connects the Canal with Yangchow. In Marco Polo's day the salt, grain, spices and silks which were traded up and down the Grand Canal were a source of wonder to the young Venetian:

> "There are very great merchants who do great trade ... they have silk beyond measure ... the most beautiful vessels of porcelain, large and small"

could be bought in the 1280's. And now? Now the canal is busier than ever. The barges on it still carry grain and silk, and now bear cement and coal to build the new China.

Entrance Numbers

The authorities devised an efficient system to transport our heavy luggage; it also was used to keep track of us as inmates of Yangchow. Everyone had an entrance number starting with an initial 10, 12, 14 or 16. After the initial number came a slash, and then a running number in family groups. Our camp representative, George Grant, among the first to arrive, was 10/1. The second batch contained the Piper family, with Mr. Piper as 12/1, his wife as 12/2, and daughter Beryl 12/3. The accounts which state that all 600 of us arrived on the same day are mistaken. Some two or three days elapsed between the arrival of one group and the next.

The first group had few families, apart from the four members of the Goodman family: Zena and her younger brother John (10/78), and their parents. An engineer, Alec Glass, later to be housed in the church at Yangchow, as we were, was there with his daughter, Moira (10/274).
The next batch to arrive were those with an initial 12 for their entrance numbers including the Pipers, as aforesaid, and the two young Martins, Keith and his sister June, along with their young cousin Peter Jewell

(12/69). Peter's mother – Mrs. "Brownie" Jewell was the adult with these youngsters. The Jewish Nissim clan was in this second group, too, as were the four Mains: Duncan Main, accompanied by his wife and two teenage daughters, Marjorie and Joan. Duncan Main was an old China hand, since Dr. David Main, his father, had run the CMS hospital at Hangchow for 45 years. [8]

A large party assembled in the grounds of Shanghai Cathedral on 15th March 1943. Our own family was in this group; our entrance numbers all began with 14: Harold, my father was 14/59; Mary, my mother 14/60, while Peter and I were 14/61 and 14/62 respectively. At the outset of this research, David Bolton asked whether I could remember my own camp number. I had quite forgotten, until my brother reminded me of it. Each piece of luggage had to be marked with a camp number. A heavy wooden box, metal-lined, remains in our family. Its white number, which my father painted on in 1943, is still clearly visible.

The Boltons, Dr. Ralph, Eileen, his wife, and their sons, Tom and David, were in this group too, as were the Azachee family and Mrs. Westwood with her teenage daughter Fay. The large Manley clan numbered fourteen all together; there were two brothers, with their wives, and two widowed sisters: Mrs. Mary Veir, and Mrs. Elizabeth Willis, together with eight children. [9]

The last group, which left Shanghai on 18th March, reached Yangchow the following day. Their journey was marked by "horrible storms and bitter cold" according to young Rosemary Green:

> "Played on deck. At 10 a.m. boarded barges for Yangchow. Went up the Grand Canal. Sharing room with the Frasers."

So Rosemary wrote. Her friend, Brenda Smith, with Brian, her younger brother, and their mother were all in this group, too. All of these had entrance numbers beginning with an initial 16; for instance Brenda's number was 16/32, her brother Brian's was 16/31 and Rosemary Green's was 16/42.[10]

Arriving in groups of some 150 to 200 individuals every few days was a system which worked well, since new arrivals could be greeted by those already there. Chris Willis records:

> "They [the first consignment] knew we were coming, and most kindly had saved enough boiling water from their own slender allowance to give us each a cup of tea. How welcome that was!"

Only after that initial greeting did we disperse to our various billets: ours in the south attic of the hospital house.[11]

Yangchow: Three Camps

Our camp, Yangchow C, was the third C.A.C. to be set up on mission property in the city. The two earlier camps – A with 375 people and B with a further 300 – only lasted a matter of months. Initially all three camps had the same commandant – Yamashita – and were interdependent in two senses. First, our bakery in Camp C made the bread for all internees in Yangchow – about 1275 people in total. Further, both A and B had medical missionaries belonging to the L.M.S., our own mission, apart from the four doctors at Camp C. Camp A had Dr. Geoffrey Milledge, and B had Dr. Geoffrey Gale and Dr. Kenneth McAll. Frances McAll, his wife, was also a qualified doctor, but had a very young daughter to care for at the time. All the missionary doctors knew one another to a degree; they would consult and aid one another where necessary. It is not surprising that the Japanese were kept busy with requests for one or other doctor from A to visit C with the benefit of his expert advice, or *vice versa*. Last of all, people from A and B made their reluctant way to Camp C for treatment at the hands of Dr. Riddell, the only dental surgeon at Yangchow.[12]

A single instance will suffice: Dr. Gell, together with Keith Gillison, the surgeon; Owen Beynon, the pharmacist, and senior nurse Wheal – all from C – visited both Camps A and B in April 1943, very soon after C camp was established. [13]

The commandant also permitted Bishop Wellington to come from B, to preside over the impressive confirmation ceremony of fourteen young candidates, in the summer of 1943. [14]

However, the three camps at Yangchow only existed in this form till September 1943. Then, the authorities arranged for some American civilians from Shanghai to be repatriated, in exchange for some Japanese from the U.S.A. This left a number of vacancies in the Shanghai camps. The 600 people from Camps A and B were fitted into these vacancies. The two early camps ceased to exist; only those of us in Yangchow C were to remain there until liberation. [15]

One final point. No-one who recalls our reaching Yangchow remembers any sense of fear; there was some apprehension of a totally unknown way of life, but no feeling that the Japanese would torture us or otherwise maltreat us. Internment was to be tough, and test the adaptability of us all, but fear was absent when we reached Yangchow.

1. HFW, 15 March 1943
2. Cyril Mack, recollections, October 2002
3. Angus, *White Pagoda*, p.108
4. Cyril Mack, recollections, October 2002
5. Brenda Smith, recollections, October 2002
6. Cyril Mack, recollections, October 2002
7. HFW, 16 March 1943 and Willis, p.59. Letter from Chris Willis to relatives in Canada, 30 September 1945.
8. Information of the Main family from Ken Flemons, husband of Joan Main, March 2003, and S. D. Sturton, *From Mission Hospital to Concentration Camp*, p.18
9. Gilbert Manley: family tree, recollections, September 2002
10. Rosemary Green, diary, 18/19 March 1943 and Brenda Smith, recollections, October 2002
11. G. C. Willis, *I was among the Captives*, p.60
12. Cliff, pp.57-8; Gillison, p.163; Frederick Jones of ABCIFER, recollections of dental treatment, July 2002
13. HFW, 21 April 1943
14. HFW, 18 July 1943
15. Cliff, pp.51 and 61

FOOD GLORIOUS FOOD

Nothing was more important to all of us in Yangchow than food. The amount and standard of food issued to us was of paramount importance. Every single person who has been in touch with me recalls Same Old Stew. Many internees had enjoyed fairly affluent life-styles in Shanghai before internment. In March 1945, no-one knew how long the war would last. Nor could anyone guess how debilitated most people would be, by the time we left Yangchow for 'home' in the autumn of 1945. Many were exhausted and readily caught infections; some had long-lasting health problems.

In general the food provided by the Japanese was inadequate. If it had not been for the Red Cross parcels which arrived from time to time, many people could have been severely under-nourished. These parcels had such significance in our lives that I have given them a section of their own. As for the regular meals for which the camp authorities were officially responsible, we can reconstruct the monotonous diet each day brought.

Breakfast consisted of one of two cereals. In summer there was 'congee', in winter a form of cracked wheat porridge. A small loaf of bread, baked on campus, was also provided. Congee was rice porridge, of a thin gruel-like consistency. Cracked-wheat porridge gave a different start to the day. This was sometimes burnt, having stuck to the bottom of the huge metal cauldron in which it was cooked. The burnt crusts were, to my mind, unappetising in the extreme. Others thought differently:

> "I did like the burnt rice from the edge of the cauldron – I suppose because it was something to chew." [1]

As for the cracked wheat, according to Keith Martin, the Canadian Red Cross had taken pity in 1938, on the people of China who were facing starvation. The Chinese had been sent huge quantities of cracked wheat. Unfortunately, the Chinese did not like this cereal so the cracked wheat ended up in store, in Shanghai. Moreover the Japanese did not permit its distribution to the most needy parts of China in the period just after 1938. By 1943, the Red Cross was sending the cereal to civilian camps in the vicinity of Shanghai. The cracked wheat porridge had the added charm of providing extra protein, in the form of weevils – dead ones. I had to shut my eyes very tightly, and gulp my porridge down. [2]

Same Old Stew appeared for tiffin, our mid-day meal. It was served from buckets. If there was any meat it was generally pork – half a pig shared between more than 600 people. Occasionally there was buffalo meat, a welcome source of protein, as Walford G. and David B. recall. A single helping of meat was about an inch long. Vegetables formed the bulk of the stew: yams, spinach, sweet potatoes, marrow or cabbage – cheap vegetables, often rotting and so needing a good deal of preparation before they could vanish into the big cauldrons. Rice too was cooked in these cauldrons, known as "ko". These served a dual purpose in camp; they were also used to sterilise surgical instruments. [3]

A team of campers prepared the unappetising vegetables. Often the cooks would commandeer as much as they could of the best food for themselves or their friends: a legitimate perk in the eyes of some campers. But grabbing of food in this fashion was enough to provoke serious protest from other campers, to the Camp committee:

> "When the committee … heard about what was going on they decided to improve the locking and policing of the kitchen. … [they] asked George Henderson, a missionary sent out by the Scottish Bible Society, if he would take on the job [of supervising the kitchen]. He agreed to do so and there was a big improvement." [4]

This was a considerable tribute to Henderson; the committee had confidence in him and so, too, had his fellow-internees.

It's fascinating to observe the change in comments on Yangchow food in my father's diary:

"Food here unexpectedly good" was his initial judgment. [5] He quickly altered his viewpoint, and criticised the long queues in which we had to stand, if we wished to eat.

"No tea today and a very inadequate supper" was his comment less than a week later. Peter and I ran across the compound each morning to fetch our family's breakfast. Often we had to put up with long waits for our porridge, described by my father as having the consistency of cement. [6]

The food queues soon formed part of the camp's social life. Fay Westwood, later in life Fay Angus, used the food queue to become acquainted with my father, who taught her history:

> "As both our surnames started with 'W', we shared the same group call to meals. I soon made a point of trying to jostle myself into a position behind him in the food queues. Here we could further develop a thought begun in the class discussions …" [7]

Of course, queues were an inevitable part of war-time life, whether in Yangchow C, or at home in England, waiting for the rations. But it's unlikely that those in England could record nothing but bread and water for evening meal, as my father did. And this was less than a month after we had entered the camp. Of course, queuing meant that each person could see the size of the helping given to the camper just ahead of him; this was a matter of some importance if you were a teenager, with a teenager's healthy appetite. [8]

Yangchow Years

Many POWs had brought supplies of tinned food with them, at the outset, to eke out the official provender. For example:

> "My parents had contrived to pack some tinned food inside the beds, which proved an enormous boon to supplement our diet over the coming years." [9]

Keith Martin's aunt, Mrs Jewell, had supplied her nephew with cash, before leaving Shanghai, so he could buy stocks of tinned food, to bring into camp. Stores like these alleviated the boredom of 'Same Old Stew'. Red beans aroused mixed reactions among the young boys in camp. David Bolton found them "too revolting to eat" while Peter Gibson reacted more favourably, recalling "those filling but cloying red beans". [10]

As far as drinks were concerned, there was no alcohol, at least until the end of the war. Tea, if you could secure the hot water in your thermos, was green tea, without milk.

The lack of milk was a serious concern to those who had young children, and also to the camp's medical staff. Keith Gillison and Ralph Bolton belonged to both of these groups, Keith with his 8 year old son Walford, and Ralph, with sons Tommy and David, of similar age. In Hankow, LMS missionaries had risen very early so as to make soya-bean milk. This was in 1942, before internment. So that children could have milk for breakfast, parents had risen at 5 a.m. to grind up the soya beans. The flavour of soya-bean milk was strongly aromatic. So too in Yangchow, it was Keith Gillison and my father who revived the practice of grinding soya beans.

The flavour of goats' milk was equally pungent. This was exclusively intended for the camp's children. The nanny goat had a smelly partner: an awesome billy. Soon there was an enchanting pair of snow-white kids: Rex and Regina. These were the first newborn creatures I had ever seen. They made a strong impression: the scarlet ribbons someone had tied around their necks, which contrasted with the brilliant white of their fleece.

> "Some of the goats had names to reflect our interest in war commanders like Monty. They were the closest we had to pets, but that did not stop some of them being eaten towards the end of the war, to bolster the meat supply." [11]

We certainly never drank goats' milk in quantity, usually half a small cup at a time. In general the amount one received varied according to one's age, so that younger children, more in need of calcium, were given more than those slightly older. Walford Gillison, aged 8, had a small cupful once a week or sometimes once in ten days.

Our bread supply depended on the camp bakery: flour, yeast and an oven were supplied. A team of bakers became skilful at the work. Baking bread was a large-scale operation as there were 610 people in Yangchow C alone (figures from March 1944). Camp C also supplied bread to the other two Yangchow camps, A and B, until their occupants were moved to Shanghai in September 1943. [12]

Apparently the ration of bread for each person was two slices. [13] Sometimes the supply of yeast failed. Echoing Marie Antoinette, my father wrote in astonishment:

> "No bread but cake!" Soon he explained "Yeast has come at last so there will be bread tomorrow after a 5 days' stoppage of bakery." [14]

The bread was far less palatable if sourdough had to be substituted for yeast. Sometimes the loaves became smaller than usual if flour supplies dwindled. We had a period from February 1944 onwards when the loaves were only 12 oz. in weight. But this did not last very long. By

May 1945 when all food supplies were running very low, we were receiving extra bread as there was no rice. [15]

When there was bread, the kitchen issued us with lard, and brawn, as spreads. The brawn was made from pigs' trotters, and from the pigs' heads; according to the camp wags, nothing of the pig was wasted, except the 'oink'.

Peanut butter was another savoury spread, home-made by putting peanuts, or ground-nuts as they were sometimes termed, through a mincer. To produce a smooth consistency, two or even three mincings were required. Peter and I fought for the privilege of turning the handle of the mincer for my mother. A very clear recollection of shelling the peanuts remains with me. Ten or twelve of us, mostly adults, sat round in a circle, with a common dish in the centre, to hold the shelled nuts. We children were carefully positioned between the adults, who were supposed to see that we ate only the allotted ration. You cracked the outer woody shell, slipped off the deep pink papery coating, and cast your nut into the common dish. Three peanuts, in every hundred shelled, was the allotted ration, and only three.

Jam tomorrow in Lewis Carroll's splendid phrase. In one sense that was what camp life was all about: looking forward to the end of the war, and to returning home. But there was jam, if we were prepared to make it ourselves. The splendid mulberry tree in the compound provided enough fruit for anyone who wished to pick the berries. My mother, like many another, made the jam, using sugar for which the cigarettes which came in Red Cross parcels will have been bartered. Once the tomatoes were produced she made another variety of jam from the small golden pear-shaped fruit grown in our family's vegetable plot. Mother took her turn cooking the meals for everyone in the camp kitchen. When this was done, people could do their own "private" cooking; making jam fell into this category. My father's contribution was to pick the mulberries, and the tomatoes, too. [16]

Eggs were occasionally brought into camp by Chinese coolies, along with other supplies, on handcarts. My mother made egg sandwiches including amaranth leaves, to provide vitamins: A, B and C, we were told. Eggs were also needed for the special occasion cakes, baked only when dried fruit and nuts reached us from the Red Cross parcels. One Russian lady, accustomed to the munificence of Imperial Russian Society, ordered "Throw in another dozen eggs" to a cake-mixture destined for Easter festivities. Such extravagance!

Vegetables grown in the garden plots near the playing field eked out the monotonous diet which was all the Japanese provided. Our plot gave us melons – but only two of them – lots of cucumbers, radishes, lettuce, and tomatoes both red and yellow. The Japanese Commandant provided the tomato seeds. [17]

It's probable that some internees, more farsighted than the rest of us, had brought seeds in with them, on arriving in March 1943. Two Red Cross letters sent to my aunt in Newcastle-on-Tyne survive; one of them sacrifices a few precious words to tell her of our success with melons and tomatoes. [18]

The camp kitchen was staffed by teams of ladies; in camp females outnumbered males. There were 304 women to 208 men, if we are to trust the camp list. A number of these women were, in the Japanese delightfully inapposite terminology "loose women". By this our captors meant either that they were unmarried, or else were unattached, since their menfolk were absent, either serving in the forces, interned elsewhere, or else missing for unknown reasons. So there were plenty of women available to deal with the cooking and the interminable vegetable preparation arranged on a rota basis, just like the other fatigues. They had to cook on stoves fuelled by coal, or failing that, wood. How long each kitchen shift lasted I have been unable to find out. Many women found the heat exhausting, especially in the high temperatures and humidity of summer in Central China. My mother never wrote about camp life, nor did Peter and I hear anything of her stints in the communal kitchen. But she did, on one occasion, collapse from exhaustion after 7½ hours' "private cooking" – that is work done just for our small family. It is not surprising: the temperature was 98°F in the shade. And she will not have been the only woman to exhaust herself in this fashion. [19]

The group of Jewish families maintained separate cooking facilities throughout the years of internment, to keep their utensils 'kosher', in accordance with Jewish custom. And of course they did not eat pork – another reason for their needing to be separate. Instead, the Jews were given extra vegetable rations.

The hospital kitchen was one of the best places to work in Yangchow C. Patients obviously needed special light diets; ladies who prepared food for the sick, might use the hospital kitchen in their own time, for private cooking. Zena Goodman's mother belonged to this group of ladies. She was evidently an experienced cook since Zena's diary records highlights of the festive dishes made there for special occasions: curry patties, salmon loaf, and the baking of special cakes, one of them a chocolate cake for Mr Goodman's birthday. Salmon, chocolate: the Goodman goodies depended on ingredients saved from the parcels received by their family. They were fortunate in having the use of the hospital kitchen.

If Zena's diary was the only source for our knowledge of the Yangchow diet, one might conclude that we lived very well indeed, like fighting cocks, in my father's graphic phrase. But the salmon loaf and chocolate cake were special, only noted by Zena because they were so different from normal food. Zena writes, too, of the meatless days, and of watery stew with its endless refrain of turnip, sweet potato and cabbage stalks. The worst combination for Zena was spinach and rice: *"Dreadful"* was her verdict, though she did concede that the camp pilau could sometimes be quite tasty. [20] By the last summer of the war, food supplies were running very low. This affected the Japanese, as well as ourselves.

Young men in their late teens or early twenties suffered from hunger probably worse than the rest of us.

> "Some growing lads in their teens actually went weeping to bed." [21]

It is not surprising that such young men were so hungry. After all, anyone over 16 did the heavy manual work of the fatigues: stoking, carrying water, or dealing with garbage disposal. Some adult smokers were prepared to exchange an egg, so they could have a few more cigarettes, to the astonishment of Keith Martin. [22] Nor is it surprising that the scent of hot loaves from the bakery proved too much for some lads, who stole the odd loaf, when they could seize their chance. [23]

Each family unit in camp had an account at the canteen, from which we could obtain Ruby Queen cigarettes, peanut brittle: a crunchy confection, and other non-essentials. "Canteen" Brown – not to be confused with "Incinerator Brown" - ran the canteen, with help from others.

The accounts were funded from Comfort allowances sent by our governments via the Red Cross. So we never handled any currency in Yangchow at all. [24]

The canteen was not open all the time, but only when the goods were available. That was not very often; we heard about it on the efficient bush telegraph which operated throughout the camp. [25]

By the summer of 1945, the prospect of starvation loomed over the camp. Just three days after a consignment of parcels arrived, Hashizumi, the Japanese commandant, announced a possible food shortage to the assembled internees, as we stood in the heat and dust of summer roll-call.

> "We might have to endure a protracted (!) siege, and go short of food." [26]

Who would besiege us? Chinese Communists, probably, as guerrillas.

It was clear that a Spartan diet could do wonders for the overweight. The medical staff could see that a restricted diet of rice porridge, a little bread, small portions of meat, and that usually masked by an unappetising stew, mostly turnips, would be good for the figure. So, too, was regular exercise, as part of the fatigue duty. Some Shanghai businessmen, very prosperous prior to internment, lost weight; they had needed to do this, as they had been very overweight on entering camp.

> "They had not enjoyed such good health for many years." [27]

Moreover, being deprived of alcohol for 2½ years will have helped them gain a svelte outline.

In the photographs taken after V.J. day in 1945, we all appear thin and tired. Many people had been ill, chiefly with malaria or dysentery. The poor diet must have contributed to the general debility. Many parents will have deprived themselves of food, so their children could have enough to eat. At one time there had been second helpings of food occasionally, and this had been eaten up by hungry teenagers. But latterly there was no spare food. The IRC parcels were necessary to our wellbeing, while the end of the war came none too soon.

[1] Brenda Smith, recollections, October 2002
[2] Keith Martin, recollections, July 2002; also Grace Harvey, recollections, 2002
[3] Walford Gillison and David Bolton, recollections, July 2002. June Martin, recollections, June 2002. For the instrument sterilising, Keith Gillison, *The Cross and the Dragon*, p.162.
[4] Gillison, op. cit., p.165
[5] HFW, 18 March 1943
[6] HFW, 24 March and 14 April 1943
[7] Angus, *White Pagoda*, p.138
[8] HFW, 5 April 1943 and Keith Martin, unpublished memoir, p.13
[9] Peter Gibson, recollections, September 2002
[10] Peter Gibson, recollections, September 2002
[11] Peter Gibson, recollections, September 2002
[12] Cliff, op. cit. (1988), p. 61
[13] Keith Martin, unpublished memoir, p.12
[14] HFW, 18 and 20 July 1943
[15] HFW, 27 May 1945 and Gillison, op. cit., p.160
[16] HFW, 2 June 1943
[17] Gillison, op. cit., p.164
[18] Comité Internationale de la Croix-Rouge, letter 136989, 29 June 1944, penes P.R.W.
[19] HFW, 25 June 1945
[20] These two paragraphs depend entirely on Zena Goodman's diary, passim
[21] George Henderson, letter to Mr. Chisholm of Bible Society, August 1945
[22] Keith Martin, unpublished memoir, p.15
[23] Brian Smith, recollections, September 2002
[24] One may contrast the way in which comfort allowances were used at Haiphong Rd., as described in Hugh Collar's book, *Captive in Shanghai*, pp.84-6.
[25] Keith Martin, recollections, October 2002
[26] HFW, 5 June 1945
[27] Walford Gillison, recollections, June 2002

WATER

> "I must be clean … Tom lay down … and looked into
> the clear limestone water, every pebble at the bottom
> bright and clean."   Charles Kingsley, *The Water Babies*

It was not easy to be clean in Yangchow. Water was often in short supply; baths were luxuries. My father's reference to "a good bath in showers for once" shows the experience was exceptional.

Water Supply

We had three sources of water. It could be wheeled in on barrows, from outside. Also, there were wells within the compound, and eventually a concrete reservoir. Nevertheless the defects in the water-supply were a major cause of complaint during internment, and also subsequently, in the 1947 enquiry regarding the 'war-guilt' of Hashizumi and Tanaka. [1]

Chinese coolies brought in water in barrels affixed to their wheelbarrows; they arrived with a high-pitched screech as the wooden wheel axles rubbed against their wooden bearings. Storage in vast kongs allowed sediment to settle; then alum and chlorine were used to purify it. Soon a reservoir was constructed to hold water pumped from the Grand Canal. This water had already been used by the Chinese living on the Canal banks. The pump frequently broke down, so the authorities reverted to the barrow system. Water was, often, short.

Two periods of severe shortage occurred in early 1944, and again in spring 1945. The first shortage began in late 1943: the outside pump broke, and was not mended till February. Only one well was functioning. Finally men and boys took buckets outside, presumably under guard. Ironically, at Chinese New Year, January 1944, there was teeming rain, so the ground was waterlogged. But hot water for bathing was only available in February, the first for six weeks. [2]

Probably this was the occasion when two internees, R. Cook and W. H. Taylor, mended the outside pump at night, as the Japanese either could not, or would not mend it themselves. [3]

Water was short again in November 1944; again the pump failed, and no barrows came in. Men carried water from outside through the East gate, my father amongst them. The shortage was most desperate throughout early 1945. Internees felled trees, to provide fuel for the pump. But it could not generate steam using wood. Coal was unobtainable. Without coal the electricity supply was cut, compounding our hardships. Teams of men spent much of the day supplying water for the kitchen. We were rationed to a scanty two quarts daily. No wonder Albert Nissim recalls

"the weekly necessity of ice-cold baths." [4]

Wells

The well, locked at night, was unlocked several times a day by Japanese guards. About ten buckets could be filled from the 3 feet of water in it, each time the well was unlocked. Each person ensured he was beside his own bucket when his turn came. [5]

A disastrous fire practice alerted the authorities to the acute shortage. On investigation, a disused well was found to have the skeleton of a Chinese solider, with rifle, at the bottom. Commandant Hashizumi permitted the digging of another well by the camp's young men. Among these was Dennis Savage. Other diggers had to rescue him, when the sandy soil caved in. This new well, situated behind House 3A was brick-lined. On completion in December 1944 it virtually doubled the water-supply. [6]

Campers became thrifty as they used precious water. Mary Savage records people using water in three or four ways, before sprinkling it on vegetable plots, or watering plants. Nonetheless, it is astonishing how many photographs show people wearing white: the Mermaids softball team sported white, and we Brownies wore white skirts and blouses. The camp ladies rose to the challenge, as Africans do today, taking pride in their families' appearance. Frances Henderson did washing for aged Mr. Milward, their colleague from the Scottish Bible Society; others will have helped those too frail to do their own laundry. [7]

Rainwater was a further resource: storms, often at night, brought heavy rain splashing into big kongs, or collected in the hospital roof-tank. Once the hospital's needs had been satisfied, men on duty distributed water from it as one of the fatigues. Obviously the hospital could not go short of water, so the Night Hawk gang of teenage lads made a chain of buckets to fill its internal water-tank on the top floor. This meant roughly half an hour's intensive co-ordinated work. [8]

Hot Water

Twice a day people collected boiling water to brew tea from the hot-water shop, behind the dining-room, near the camp wall. Usually we took thermos flasks; a broken flask was tragic, since replacement was difficult. Sometimes the canteen sold new flasks; my father secured two, costing $800 each. [9]

Scalding was a frequent hazard, when people brought unsuitable containers. When the supply was lowest, hot water was rationed: three cups per person, per day. We queued when the temperature was only 18°F, and got three-quarters of a thermos for the four of us, in January 1945. Those in the Bakery team could sometimes have a jug of hot water as an extra perk. This caused bitterness among other internees, in the extreme cold of February 1945.

Messrs. Glass and Mulvey engineered the hot-water supply, with strips of piping, à la Heath Robinson. Unsophisticated this may have been, but camp morale would have been infinitely lower without the tonic effect of a mug of tea, warm to the fingers in the bitter cold. [10]

If distributing water at times of shortage was one of the men's fatigues, so too was transporting waste water. Keith Martin recollects carrying water upstairs to the room he shared with relatives; naturally all the waste had to be lugged downstairs in pails. [11]

As for the bath house, the authorities had long despaired of using it for its proper purpose, as it was too far from most of our accommodation. Halfway through internment it was converted for the Belgians, who arrived in November 1944. One of them, Mme. Geneviève Ley, claimed it was quite unsuitable as a billet, especially for women and children. It was very damp, cold and draughty, infested with rats in winter, and mosquitoes in summer. [12]

Water was as vital to our survival as food, if only because of the climatic extremes of central China. Summer temperatures regularly climbed well over 100°F; in winter they dropped well below freezing. Water kept overnight in billets froze solid, in winter months. Yangchow C was, as far as I know, the only CAC to suffer such severe problems of water-supply – a point stressed by the ex-internee witnesses against Hashizumi and Tanaka in 1947.

Sanitation

Our loos were one of the most horrible features of Yangchow. They stank; children and adults alike were apprehensive about using them. They were located in buildings separate from our houses; this involved a chilly walk if one needed to use them at night. There were individual cubicles, with seats over lidded buckets. Urinals for the men smelt, especially in summer. They were open to the many flies. The latrines were divided into men's and women's sections. The church had no loo behind it, so people living there generally used the loo that was adjacent to House 2.

Chinese amahs – nicknamed Glamour Girls – emptied the thunderboxes into wooden tubs, which swung at each end of the bamboo pole carried on the amah's shoulders. The Glamour Girls emptied the tubs via a drain running through the wall, behind the laundry. The contents were collected outside the camp, to be spread on the fields as fertiliser by the thrifty Chinese. When there was sufficient water the Glamour Girls gave the buckets a cursory rinse with a bamboo whisk. The camp medics. inspected the buckets regularly checking for evidence of disease, so as to prevent outbreaks of dysentery, or other complaints. Possibly Keith Gillison was engaged on this inspection, when Fay Westwood thought he was cleaning the latrines. [13]

This primitive situation was believed to contribute to the bouts of dysentery suffered by many people. The evidence provided by former internees against Hashizumi stresses this point. Smell is often evocative in human memory. Even now a whiff of poorly maintained drains carries me over the years, straight back to those unlovely latrines. [14]

[1] WO 325/122 in P.R.O.
[2] HFW entries for 25, 27 and 29 January, also 4 February 1944
[3] W. H. Taylor's evidence in WO 325/122 in P.R.O. Most ex-internees supplying evidence in 1947 stressed Yangchow's inadequate water supply.
[4] HFW, 14 November 1944; also 20 January, 20 February, 5 March 1945. Albert Nissim, recollections, December 2002
[5] K. Gillison, p.159
[6] K. Gillison, p.164, Mary Savage, unpublished memoir, p.7. HFW 19 November and 3 December 1944. The discovery of the soldier's skeleton is told in Leslie Green's unpublished account
[7] George Henderson, letter to Mr. Chisholm, 20 August 1945
[8] For the Night Hawks, see Owen Manley, recollections, October 2002
[9] HFW, 19 August 1944
[10] Angus, p.117, Owen Manley, recollections, October 2002, and Willis, p.97
[11] Keith Martin, unpublished memoir, p.12
[12] Evidence of Mme. Ley, Q-form in WO 325/122, in the P.R.O.
[13] Angus, p.134
[14] For the evidence against Hashizumi see WO 325/122 in P.R.O.

CLOTHING

"Behold I make all things new"

Clothing or rather the lack of appropriate clothes became a serious problem. Worn out clothes could not be replaced. Mothers of growing children – nearly a hundred of us – resorted to barter to clothe their children, or to what we now term recycling, which was only common sense. Neil Begley states that flour bags were remade into shirts and blouses. Eventually warm clothing received from the Red Cross came to the rescue.

Knitting was a favoured occupation for the women folk, as old jumpers were refashioned into new garments. A lack of knitting-needles was soon put right as Myfanwy Beynon's boyfriend slivered up bamboo to make Van a set of four needles. She knitted gloves and mittens for herself and her friends, against the bitter cold. Knitting came into its own with the new babies first in the Taylor family, and then to Lilee Cook and her husband.[1]

Clothes Exchange

Common sense dictated that outgrown clothes be exchanged, so younger children could inherit them. Much of this was done informally, between friends. But Kath Gillison, teacher and wife to the camp surgeon, and Salvationist Edith Begley established a weekly Sale and Exchange shop. Vendors brought in clean clothes and shoes, and decided the value of the goods themselves. Cigarettes formed the camp currency: a shirt could be 22 cigarettes, or some shoes in good repair 28. Ironically neither lady smoked.[2]

Mothers did many a private deal over their children's clothes. In Rosemary Green's journal an interesting equation appears, during the last summer of our internment. Val Judah, who played Portia in *The Merchant of Venice* was older than Rosemary, and their mothers were friendly. Three of Val's dresses, a playsuit and two petticoats were equivalent to the nightdress, blouse, pair of shorts and two pairs of pants which Mrs. Green gave Mrs. Judah. The deal was concluded with a final kilo of peanuts from the Green family.

By this time we had been in camp for more than two years. Mothers were at their wits' end, as to how to clothe their growing youngsters. Their anxiety was somewhat relieved when a consignment of clothing arrived via the Red Cross. There were garments for men and women, but fewer clothes for youngsters. A blouse and pair of slippers, together with two sets of underwear fell to Mrs. Green's lot, while her daughter only received a blouse. Later it was the turn of boys and men; 12 year old Leslie Green had to be content with a pair of slippers, and his father had stockings, singlets and other underwear, as well as a pair of rubber shoes.[3]

Hand-me downs and borrowed plumes

In Shanghai days, taipans might have despised the custom of passing clothes down from elder to younger child. But now we were all on the same level, so younger brothers and sisters came in for the garments of their elders, who, in turn, awaited cast-offs from adults.

A fair amount of borrowing went on, for special occasions. The journals of Beryl Piper and Zena Goodman are, naturally, full of the outfits the girls wore to Saturday evening dances: "Joan wore her blue" is a typical entry. Frocks or skirts were loaned, to be returned later, just as Beryl Piper needed to borrow a white skirt for the School Certificate presentation in August 1944.

Many mothers cut up garments from their own wardrobes, to make "new" clothes for their teenage daughters. This was true of most CAC's: Mrs. Box, mother to Phyllis and Eleanor, had thought ahead sufficiently to take some rolls of cotton cloth into camp with her, so she and her two girls could have new clothes. [4]

People rose to the challenge imposed by difficult circumstances. The poor water supply brought out our latent obstinacy. The general attitude was:

"We'll try to look presentable, whatever the difficulty."

Hence we Brownies had to wear white, just as the nursing staff of the hospital did: Matron Wheal, Nurse Jagger and the part-time staff, such as Hilda Shepherd, and Mrs Jewell. Photographs of the Guides emphasise the same point.

Of course in summer we children wore as little as possible, since it was so hot: cotton sunsuits for the girls, a pair of more or less scruffy shorts for boys. The school staff must have required lads to wear shirts for lessons, but, out of school, shirts were abandoned. Adult men generally took to shorts for summer wear, as my own father did. Some men "let themselves go", in the sense that they only wore a vest with their shorts, while others always wore a shirt, though often an open-necked shirt, because of the heat. By August 1945 many pairs of shorts were patched, and patched again (see the VIth Form photo, August 1945). In the bakery and kitchen teams, men often resorted to singlets, or wore nothing at all, apart from their shorts. This is clear in the photos of bakery teams or kitchen squads which survive.

In the summer heat it was far more important to wear a hat, the wide brimmed variety, against the sun. The old-fashioned topee was worn by a few men but more often they sported wide brimmed cotton hats, like those now worn by cricketers. Many children had pull-on cotton headgear, or straw sunhats with huge brims to shield their necks. Girls in the kitchen often wore turbans, all the rage from the fashion angle.

Professionals made efforts to keep their uniforms trim. The photograph of medical staff taken in August 1945 shows them clad in aertex shirts, the nurses in white uniforms, as smart as can be. As for the clerics, Rev. P. C. Matthews had his white surplice, laundered for him by Mrs. Jewell, over his cassock on Sundays. My father wore his Edinburgh M.A. gown for services; he only used its white hood at Christmas and Easter. Where Anglican tradition prescribed a black stole round the neck, Dad's stole was ivory silk, and like his hood, reserved for festal days. Years before, some Chinese ladies had embroidered it for him; it had a gold cross at one hand, and a fiery burning bush in flame and scarlet at the other. I thought it was gorgeous.

One way to enliven drab clothing, for the women at least, was wearing jewellery, not valuable jewels of course, but handmade brooches and bracelets. Young men often spent their leisure fashioning boxes or beads, using their penknives. The female gingko tree, which figures so large in the memories of so many of us, produced nuts which could be made into ornamental buttons. Two holes for the thread were pierced in the sides; the nuts were then buried under some leaves for a time. They turned hard, light and shiny, but only after the maker had cleaned away the smelly interior. Van Beynon made herself a set of these; she used a magnifying glass and the rays of the sun to burn a pattern of little dots on to her buttons. She still cherishes a bracelet made from the hard wood of the box-tree. The bracelet is made up of seven sections: each has a single letter of her true Welsh name on it: MYFANWY. The sections were strung on elastic, with a loving message inscribed inside. Joan Beynon, known to the young chaps who liked her as 'Bunny' was given a flat wooden rabbit to act as bookmark by her elder sister Van. In their odd minutes the stokers fashioned privet wood into delicate initial brooches; Fay Westwood was gratified to be one of the few girls to receive one of these.[5]

What tools did they use? Ingenuity made the young men find pieces of sharp broken glass, to smooth the wood. Broken needles became tiny chisels. The end was sharpened on a stone, and the point stuck into a homemade wooden handle. [6]

Corduroy

Corduroy was the material which kept out the cold in severe weather. Red Cross parcels contained cord trouser suits in brownish-orange, "cod-liver oil suits", to use Neil Begley's terminology. Their strange colour reminded the youngsters of that loathsome medicine. The jackets were cut in battledress style, and had orange flannel linings, so warm one girl went to bed in hers. Men had orange plus-fours from the Red Cross. Owen Manley delighted in the extra winter warmth, compared to the shorts he had always worn previously. Winter began in earnest when my father resurrected his old corduroy bags. Sometimes he, too, sported plus-fours, tucked into long wool stockings. A black beret – Monty style – completed his winter outfit. So cold was it in December 1944 that he was still shivering, despite wearing one coat on top of another. [7]

Parachutes

Despite perpetual washing, patching and darning, we were a scruffy lot when first U.S. and then British forces came to our rescue. Fortunately the American parachute drops relieved our parlous state. Clothing from them included pale khaki waterproof wind-cheaters, with many, many pockets, zip-fastened, as well as badly-needed footwear. Best of all, the parachutes themselves made luxury garments in the newest of fabrics.

Parachute nylon, fine and tough, was a magic manmade fabric. Women prized it; they ran up new frocks and underwear from the high quality stuff. A shimmering white waist-slip was made for me; it lasted many a summer. Brenda Smith was the envy of her friends at her English boarding-school for her turquoise silky dressing-gown, another ex-parachute garment. In the draw organised by the girls Fay Westwood won a whole 'chute, a vast white circle. She dreamed of a delectable wedding gown, though she had no prospective bridegroom as yet. [8]

The nylon was shared among all of us: the ration was 2/3 of a parachute each. Some internees preferred cigarettes, so non-smokers won more than their share. We, for instance, had sufficient nylon to make grass-green bedspreads, which lasted for years afterwards, a tribute to the fabric's enduring quality.

The airdrops brought boots and clothes as well as food. Owen Manley writes:

> "When we had the airdrops of U.S. Army clothing and boots, we had never experienced such luxury." [9]

Fancy Dress

Fancy dress acted as a boost to camp morale. Beryl Piper's journal is full of references to special occasions: Empire Day parades, or just Saturday evening dances; in midsummer of our first year Rosemary Green made herself an Alice in Wonderland costume, only to see her own brother Leslie win the contest along with Zena Goodman. Those who performed in camp concerts or camp fire skits dressed up of course. Keith Gillison, the camp surgeon, was helped into his stage costume by my father on more than one occasion. Young people wriggling their way through the conga on New Year's Eve 1944 had ripped the counterpanes from their beds, to wear as suitably crazy attire. At such times we were no longer prisoners of the increasingly shabby garments we brought into camp in the spring of 1943. [10]

1. Myfanwy Beynon, recollections, February 2003
2. Keith Gillison, pp. 161-2
3. Rosemary Green, 14 and 18 June 1945
4. Phyllis and Eleanor Box, recollections, June 2002
5. Van Beynon, recollections, February 2003, and Fay Angus, p. 120
6. Van Beynon, recollections, February 2003
7. Neil Begley, p. 96, June Martin, recollections June 2002, and Owen Manley, recollections, October 2002, HFW 13 December 1944
8. Brenda Smith, recollections, October 2002, and Angus, p. 154
9. Owen Manley, recollections, October 2002
10. Rosemary Green, 12 June 1943, and Beryl Piper, 31 December 1944

FOOTWEAR

> "I gotta shoes, you gotta shoes
> All God's children gotta shoes"
>
> Negro spiritual

Footwear posed a serious problem for practically all internees. For the parents of growing children, providing shoes capable of withstanding the snow, rain and mud of a Yangchow winter was taxing enough. But adults, too, could easily find their footwear falling to pieces, as the war dragged on. Though the Red Cross parcels did sometimes contain shoes, there was no guarantee that shoes of a suitable size would materialise when they were needed.

Hence, Major Begley, of the Salvation Army, was responding to a genuine need when he set himself up as the camp cobbler. Begley had brought the equipment necessary for shoe mending with him, when he entered camp. Soon he was in business, for the price of shoes in Shanghai had become excessive in 1943, owing to war-time inflation. Less prosperous internees had spent much of their cash in providing themselves with stores of tinned food. Thus some families entered camp with shoes which were good enough at the start, but which gradually wore out, as month followed month, and still the war did not end.

Early and late, through cold and heat, Major Begley sat in his corner, clad in his shoemaker's apron. His chief assistant was the unlikely figure of Sir Cyril Young, the English baronet, whose cobbling skill was excellent. A year after the war ended, Mrs. Willis still had some shoes which had been given new soles by the baronet, soles made out of discarded rubber boots. Major Begley was sometimes able to act as middle-man, in true Chinese fashion, and effect exchanges between campers. For instance,

Yangchow Years

Chris Willis himself won a good pair of shoes which had been discarded by one of the wealthy Jewish internees, and these replaced footwear which had disintegrated into inadequacy. [1]

In the school holidays Van Beynon was assistant shoemaker. Her job was to patch shoes where people's toes and bunions had rubbed through, and salvage the tongues from outworn shoes. She perched on a fat cut log outside the shoemender's hut. Her bubbly personality attracted a crowd of friends who used to drag up their own logs, so they could sit and chat to Van as she worked. It was the worst job of all to 19 year old Van, worse than teaching beginners' geography or maths under the scrutiny of older teachers, including the intimidating headmaster and headmistress. [2]

The classic method of dealing with children's growing feet was to cut the tips from their shoes. This was done in Yangchow, in Lunghua and doubtless in most other camps, too. Sand shoes were David Bolton's summer wear:

> "Miserable, canvas-topped things. Other shoes were liable to lose their heels, and I would get into trouble for not bringing them home." [3]

The lads must have played cricket and football in these ordinary shoes, since special boots were not available. As for the girls, they made attractive sandals for themselves out of spare fabric. They plaited strips of cloth, either torn from the hem of a skirt, or else made by re-using an outworn garment. The strips were made into firm soles, and attached with thongs, again made of fabric, to the feet. Sometimes boys wore these too. A final female fashion note: wooden clogs, hand-shaped, were sometimes worn. [4]

Of course, parents themselves tried their hands at cobbling. My father had tried this in Hankow, in 1942, long before we reached Yangchow. Then he had used an old bicycle tyre, to mend my brother Peter's sandals. He was still at it at the very end of the war, some 12 days before V.J. Day. [5]

> "Tried my hand at cobbling shoes for Mary and converting shoes into sandals for Peter. Not very successful!"

he commented ruefully. Many other fathers, throughout the internment camps of China, will have attempted something similar, a good example of the make-do-and-mend mentality of all internees. [6]

It was a relief for everyone when the American parcels, dropped from the B29's in September 1945 were found to contain high quality boots as well as clothing. And, as soon as the war ended, it was once again possible to get Chinese craftsmen to repair shoes, work done with skill and expedition. One of my clearest memories is one of a Chinese cobbler drawing round my foot, clad in its white sock. "Put your foot on that piece of white paper, and stand quite still!" Such was the command, and how difficult it was to obey, as the travelling pencil traced my foot's outline on the paper. It tickled.

---

[1] Willis, pp. 109-10
[2] Van Beynon, recollections, February 2003
[3] Eleanor Box from Lunghua, and David Bolton, recollections, June 2002
[4] Angus, *White Pagoda*, p. 122, Peggy Taylor, Recollections of World War II in China, unpublished memoir, p. 8
[5] HFW, 7 May 1942
[6] HFW, 3 August 1945

BILLETING

D'ye ken Yangchow and the billets there
With old Joe Evans a'tearing his hair?
If you've forty square feet and a breath of fresh air
You'd better stay put till the morning.
                    Camp song, to the tune of *John Peel*

Shared accommodation caused many problems. Afterwards, those who lived in such cramped conditions valued privacy; one young man promised himself he would never again live so close to others. We were allowed 40 square feet of space each, including access.

In some parts of Yangchow C families were only divided from one another by makeshift curtains. Elsewhere straw matting gave the illusion of walls, as in the church where our family lived.

Was it preferable to have a small self-contained room, or in a larger area, divided into cubicles? The latter gave more visual privacy, but conversations could still be heard. The church with its high Gothic vault had straw matting some six and half feet high. Conversation was never really private.

The Gillisons had a cubicle in a large room, holding 24 people. It held three folding beds, with a small table, and folding chairs:

> "One cubicle was occupied by a Catholic priest who talked loudly in his sleep, one by a lady who snored, and another by three women who were greatly alarmed if a window was left open." [1]

Sleep was difficult in these conditions. Happiness depended on chance; someone keen on fresh air hoped not to be surrounded by fug-fiends. And vice versa.

It was easier to share with relatives, as the George Manley family did, with George's two widowed sisters, Mrs. Veir and Mrs. Willis, and their children, ten in all.

> "Water froze in our room during winters"

according to Owen Manley.[2]

June and Keith Martin lived with their aunt, Mrs. Jewell and her son, Peter, as well as two unattached ladies, Jessie Ferguson, and Nell Picozzi. A close friend and her daughters made the total of nine people. Their room was divided from their friends' living-space by a "wall" of straw matting, less than half the height of the room.[3]

Keith's friend from the Cathedral School, Shanghai had originally been allocated, with his family, to Yangchow B. They and others moved to camp C so they could plan the accommodation for the groups of internees, and receive each new intake as it arrived. But arrangements made at the outset were liable to change: to absorb incomers, or to improve facilities for the entire camp. Once settled, however, people were reluctant to move; this is understandable when we recall how much disruption was involved with the process of internment.

Overcrowding, whether among humans, or in other animal populations produces signs of stress. Yangchow was a prime example of this. It was hard on everyone that most indoor conversations could be overheard: marital rows, tension between old and young, scoldings, snoring, gossip harmless and gossip malicious – all these were impossible to conceal. In summer one could always escape out of doors, to walk around the camp perimeter wall. Pairs of friends, married couples, and couples who might or might not have been courting, all walked around, often at evening time. This was impossible however in the chill Yangchow winters. As a child I had no idea that adults needed private time with one another. Many a rocky marriage will have crashed from lack of sufficient privacy to sort out a disagreement.

Initially our family was fortunate; on arrival we had a room to ourselves. The south facing attic, in the hospital house, was opposite the Beynon family's room. This Welsh family had two daughters. The elder, Myfanwy, known to the entire camp as Van, had a vivacious personality and waving red gold hair. Joan, the younger sister was quieter. Combining brains and beauty, she soon became a star in my father's history classes. Both girls were in their late teens.

Being so close to the roof, the attics were warm: an advantage it seemed, until spring came, and the warmth became oppressive. Central China has summers of intense heat, and high humidity, with temperatures rising to more than 100°F.

The house was destined to be the hospital for all three Yangchow camps. Soon the medical superintendent declared the attics were needed for night nurses. The prospect of moving filled both my parents with apprehension. We children were settled, and preferred Yangchow to Shanghai. Each day they packed us off to school, in the baggage room. [4]

After pressure from the medical superintendent, we moved to the church building, near the gate, and the Japanese headquarters. The cubicles there were intended for two people or four. A foursome was allocated two of the arched church windows and the adjoining space, while a two-person unit – husband and wife, or two friends like Betty James and Gwen Morris of the L.M.S. – had only a single window-space. [5] Foursomes were usually families: the Gibsons, with Kenneth and Peter, their sons, and the ginger-haired MacDonalds, from Scotland. Sheila MacDonald, the youngest, was one of our Gang of Four.

A married lady, Mrs. R. lived next door, with her daughter; the father was absent. Lacking paternal authority, the girl's behaviour was unruly. My parents feared her influence. Would I, too, become cheeky and disobedient? The high roof of the church resounded to her mother's remonstrances:

"You go to h---!" was the spirited riposte.

And my father's heart-felt entry in his diary:

> "Wish [the child] would go to bed and stay quiet at a decent hour." [6]

Two or three years older than I, this girl delighted in frightening me with tales of the ghosts which inhabited the church. Shadowy figures glided each night from the white stone memorial tablets on the church walls. I lay rigid in bed, unable to sleep. What would the ghosts do when they got me? Reading Charlotte Brontë's *Villette* ten years later, the power of the spectral nun was drawn from the fantasies inspired in my five year old soul in camp.

Those with a room to themselves realised their good fortune. Marjorie Train wrote:

> "Parents and myself [were] very lucky – Had our own room." [7]

The Willis family longed for privacy. Helen, Chris' sister, originally lived in the Ladies' Dorm. This was vast, and contained more than sixty females, varying in age, appearance and character. Poor Helen Willis! In these circumstances, it was impossible for her to enjoy a moment of quiet, for prayer or study. Hence, when her brother and his wife were asked to move from their airy room which suited them, to somewhere larger, Chris bargained with the billeting authorities for his sister to join them. So there were five in the new room: three Willises and an elderly married couple. Mercifully, the two groups had learnt enough tolerance to reach agreement over opening and closing of their shared window. [8]

As winter approached, the questions of opening or shutting windows became a source of tension. Shared accommodation often means difficulty over such apparently trivial matters. With hindsight, the first few months meant settling down, as internees resigned themselves to living close to other people, often very different in age, background and expectation. It was possible to change billets, hoping the new one would be more congenial than the old. The billeting officer must have attracted a good deal of unpopularity, especially when people had to live in huge dormitories.

The Ladies' Dorm. was home to Fay Westwood and her mother, for the entire 2½ years of internment. Mrs. Westwood, once an accountant for Butterfield & Swire on the Shanghai Bund, was elected Dorm. Representative, reporting to the Camp committee. Fay still has a letter of appreciation signed by all those inhabiting the dorm, women whose problems Mrs. Westwood dealt with, day by day.

The Hornets' Nest

Young bachelors were in the Hornets' Nest. It had a fearsome reputation to teenage lads like Owen Manley. If sent on an errand, boys would try to enter unobtrusively:

> "deliver our message and depart as rapidly as possible ... We were likely to be pounced upon, and our heads shaved to resemble billiard balls. Seven bald lads sat shoulder to shoulder, in the dining-room ... proud victims of the dread Hornets' Nest."

When 'Bully' Bulldeath married Nora Quincey, his former buddies, sworn bachelors, thought he was deserting them ...

> "Residents [of the Hornet's Nest] showed their disdain for one of their number succumbing to the state of matrimony by hanging his bed outside the dorm. Window."

Naturally enough, these buddies called the hut given to the newlyweds "Honeymoon Lodge".

One tale about the notorious Nest runs thus:

> "One evening after Lights Out, one of the lads loudly drags a chamber pot across the floor, and most audibly pours water into it from a great height. It's then 'accidentally' kicked over, spilling its contents, which cascaded through the floorboards onto the heads and beds of the maiden ladies below. The scramble and screams of hysteria were pitiful to hear." [9]

Accommodation probably caused more tension among our internees than any other issue, with the possible exception of food. The billeting committee's decisions always aroused criticism. For instance, during the summer of 1944 feelings were roused over the proposal to have fourteen more people in the church. Backed up by Mr. MacDonald, my father stated his view that no more children should be accommodated there. Eight youngsters: two Gibson sons, two MacDonald daughters, Joan Roach, Moira Glass, Peter and I – were already there. His view must have prevailed. The new occupants – all adults – arrived at the end of August; new partitions were erected to make cubicles for them. [10]

Later still, even more people came to join us in the church; among them was Joan Penfold, the camp headmistress and her elderly parents.

Clearly billeting was not arranged for permanency. By this late date, people knew there would be an Allied victory, and we would all leave.

Meantime many of us had had more than one 'home' – the pattern of accommodation was very fluid.

---

[1] Gillison, K. *The cross and the dragon*, p.158
[2] Owen Manley, recollections, October 2002
[3] Keith Martin, unpublished memoir, p.12
[4] HFW, 1 and 5 April 1943
[5] See the Group I photo, which shows the church's inhabitants in August, 1945. The window design is very clear.
[6] HFW, 10 June 1943
[7] Marjorie Train, letter to the author, July 2002
[8] Willis, p.61 and pp.66-8
[9] Owen Manley, recollections, October 2002
[10] HFW, 14, 19 and 23 June 1944. Also 31 August 1944.

BILLETING: PESTS

Mosquitoes

The high-pitched whine of a mosquito was a sound familiar to everyone. To this day the acrid smell of a mosquito coil, lit to keep the pests away, evokes Yangchow. Mosquitoes were feared as carriers of malaria. The most serious cases went to hospital, my mother among them. Malaria sapped her resistance; hence she was seriously ill six months after leaving Yangchow. And many others suffered likewise. Meantime in her absence, my father saw us to bed, and the nightly chase for mosquitoes trapped inside our nets began.

Fay Westwood, aged 15, valued the privacy of her bed:

> "My mosquito net was the joy of my internment ... [By day] it would swing in a huge rolled knot above my bed ... At night when it tucked me into solitude, it was my cave, my castle, my secret garden."

Even in winter, Fay insisted on keeping her mosquito net, to the derision of other girls in her dorm., valuing the illusion of privacy. I, too, recall enjoying a small space exclusively my own. [1]

Bugs

Bedbugs were a nasty hazard; most families were troubled by them. They nested in the crannies of the canvas campbeds used by many people. They infested the Chinese quilts, stuffed with cotton, which were so badly needed in winter. Our family was afflicted, too:

> "We and others are being bothered with bugs. A job to get rid of them." [2]

Someone brought a high quality spring bed with him, only to find his prized possession infected with bugs.

> "He took it outdoors, took it all to pieces and ... threw away the greater part of the bed. Dennis Savage carefully gathered up those springs, and hid them away; they were made of good quality sprung steel, and many was the needle, or awl for shoe repairs, that he made from those discarded springs." [3]

The only effective cure, to rid metal bedframes from bugs was to secure a candle, if you could, light it, and burn the nasties.

BILLETING: THE BELGIANS

Halfway through internment we heard the news: some fifty Belgians were to arrive from Tientsin. They actually arrived in mid-November 1944; only 38 in total, 22 were men or boys, and 16 women. Looked at another way, 28 were adults, and 10 were children. Two individuals stood out in this group: one enormous chap who was epileptic, liable to fall unconscious, to the alarm of those round about. Mme. Génie Delabis was blonde and attractive. [4]

The Belgian names were added in longhand to the typed list of camp members [dated 8th March 1944, provenance unknown].

The bath-house was allocated to the Belgian group as accommodation. It needed considerable alteration from the Public Works Department. This led to the Savage incident, when Tanaka, the Japanese supply officer, forced Fred Savage to kneel on the icy ground. [5]

Why the Belgians arrived at this juncture is not clear. I surmise that the Japanese considered Belgium an enemy after the D-Day landings in June 1944, and the Allied advance through Northern France and into Belgium itself. Prior to this, Belgium was occupied by Germany; its citizens in

China were no concern of the Japanese. Once Belgium was an enemy country, her citizens were interned as enemy aliens, like ourselves.

Again, why they were moved from North China, to Yangchow much further south, remains a mystery. Probably camps in North China could not accommodate them. I have no memory of Belgians at all, but Mona Nissim, my contemporary, recalls Brigitte – a Belgian girl in our age-group, about 7 years old. My attempts to trace individuals in Brussels were unsuccessful. Nor can the present authorities in Belgium shed any light on the reason for their arrival in Yangchow, in 1944.

But they did take part in camp activities, to the extent of fielding a team in the tug-of-war contest, which was part of the Empire Day celebrations in 1945. Further, the ceremony held to celebrate the end of the war included the Belgian flag, next to those of Britain, Russia, China and the United States. Internees stood at attention on parade, as each country's national anthem was played. [6]

---

[1] Angus, p.116
[2] HFW, 5 July 1945
[3] Willis, p.98; Dennis Savage confirmed this story to me, October 2002
[4] For the Belgians' arrival, see HFW 16 September and 16 November 1944. The individuals are recalled by Walford Gillison
[5] See section on the Japanese for the full story
[6] Beryl Piper, 24 May and 11 September 1945

THE COMPOUND

"Annihilating all that's made
To a green thought in a green shade."
                    Andrew Marvell, *The Garden*

Our compound was originally established by the American Church Mission. Probably its members meant to create an oasis of trees and shrubs, to remind them of home. In this respect we were fortunate, compared to those in Shanghai camps. Our isolation at Yangchow provided us with space and colour, in contrast to the far less pleasant urban conditions at Pootung, or Ash Camp.

By contrast, "a horrible place to be in" was my father's judgment on Pootung, which he visited with Peter, in late 1945, to see how his B.M.S. friend, Tom Allen, had fared during the war. [1]

"We are fortunate to live in such a compound", wrote my father, in early 1944. It was spring: he was struck by the beauty of the white snowball tree, and later on by the fine roses which hung on the porch of one of the Japanese residences. Many people from Yangchow C recall the two immense gingko trees *[Gingko biloba]* which shed their golden leaves in October. A vast magnolia grew against one of the buildings. Only later in life did I learn it was *Magnolia grandiflora*, with large creamy-white flowers. My parents called it the tulip-tree. Trumpets of deep blue morning glory grew on the north wall of the church, which was our home. A lilac was especially fine, that spring. The big mulberry with its squashy purple fruit allowed women, my mother among them, to make jam, with our meagre sugar ration. [2]

In the hot and humid summer, flowers grew in profusion at Yangchow. A Scotsman, W. A. Macdonald, was in charge of the gardens. His wife, typically Scottish with auburn hair, taught botany to our class; we learnt to distinguish pink, white and purple cosmos, and the stiff orange-red zinnias. This was easy enough, but then Mrs. Macdonald went on to talk of annuals, biennials and perennials. Whatever did these long words mean, and how could she use them with such confidence? [3]

Birds

Despite our proximity to Yangchow town just outside, the compound was a bird-lovers' paradise, with bullfinches and bulbuls, blackbirds and spotted woodpeckers. Gilbert Manley's map shows where long-tailed tits nested, in the small firs behind the commandant's house. The long avenue of elm trees was home to the rooks. A magpie nested near the incinerator in the camp's north-east corner. Being in camp so long meant we knew when to expect migrants:

> "the golden oriole has been here 2 days already"

wrote my father, in the last springtime of the war. [4]

A collection of birds' eggs and feathers has survived in Colin Henderson's family. From it we know there were doves, mynah birds and azure magpies, too. The young lads, Colin, Albert Nissim, Neil Begley and Peter Jewell among them, would go bird nesting at early dawn, despite the Camp Committee's ban on disturbing birds at nesting time. The lads collected eggs avidly:

> "we imposed our own rule: you never took more than one egg ... but that didn't limit the number of boys who each took an egg." [5]

Even the adults occasionally took part, as Gilbert Manley recalls:

"One night, we – the bird nesting fraternity caught an unexpected pair of legs descending from a rather easy dove's nest. It turned out to be an extremely embarrassed Mr. Green collecting an egg for his son, Leslie, too young, timid or awkward to do the deed himself."

Egg-collecting was then regarded as a respectable hobby. The boys' self-imposed code demanded they only took newly laid eggs, which they could blow successfully. They learnt to drill two small holes, one at each end of the egg, and then blow out the contents. [6]

Birds flew in and out, regardless of the walls which kept us prisoners. Brahminy kites nested in the tall trees near the camp's north-west corner. None of the boys possessed a kite's egg, as the nest was inaccessible to even the bravest of the bird-nesting boys. Neil Begley remembers:

"We did not dare climb to the top of the giant poplars where kites nested." [7]

One bird we missed because of our confinement was the kingfisher; Peter and I had learnt about them from our time in Siaokan – another walled town – which was our mission-station, before we left to go to Hankow. As for adults on fatigue duty, one of the rewards for a long spell of fatigue could be the sight of another bird or beast, venturing out when most of the camp was asleep. On one occasion, my father disturbed a stoat among the reeds,

"a bonny wee fellow" [8]

Gardens

In terms of our survival, the growing of vegetables in small garden plots was far more important than all enjoyment of the natural beauty which surrounded us. No-one had to garden, but many did so, from choice.

Our family had a plot; so too did the Green family. Fresh vegetables – lettuces, cucumbers and tomatoes – were an excellent change from the tired and often rotten yams and carrots which came into camp, by Japanese command. Our own crops were good to eat, and nourishing, too. People grew quantities of the normal red tomatoes; there were small golden tomatoes as well, pear-shaped. I have never encountered them since our days in Yangchow. They were tasty, and made another type of jam, to spread on such bread as we had. In the summer heat, melons and loofahs flourished too. My father took great pride in his few melons.

One of the surviving Red Cross letters sent to my aunt Sue in Newcastle lists the vegetables we grew: melons and cucumbers, as well as tomatoes and lettuce. Presumably Mother was trying to reassure her sister that we were all still alive, and could grow food on our vegetable plot. [9]

Loofahs fascinated me: how could a fat green cucumber become something which you could scrub your knees with? We watched it dry out in the sun: the skeletal structure soon became clear. Rattling the black seeds out of the loofah was my job, fun for the small girl I was then.

As for the gardeners, there is no doubt that the spells of digging and preparing the soil in the open air was good for their health. People gardened because they enjoyed the activity and the results. This kind of work was quite different from compulsory fatigues, stoking or night-patrol for the men, or the everlasting chopping of vegetables, and doing the family laundry, as far as women were concerned.

Our doctors stressed the value of the vitamins contained in the vegetables we grew, and also the fresh air and exercise involved. Some people had the foresight to bring seeds with them at the outset. Most gardeners shared their produce with others: my father's tomato plants came from the Hay family. Even Hashizumi, the Japanese commandant, is credited with obtaining tomato seeds for us. A surplus of vegetables could be shared with those who had no garden plot. Sometimes this surplus was a gift; at other times it would be bartered for other goods or services. How many tomatoes did George Henderson charge for a haircut? [10]

The long summers meant meetings, classes and church services could be held out-of-doors, usually in the shade, for temperatures could rise to more than 100°F; indeed the thermometer rose to 102.3°F, according to Owen Beynon, on one July day. It was all too easy to catch a touch of the sun. But even the choir preferred to practise outside in summer, away from the stuffiness indoors. [11]

We ate out-of-doors too: tiffin, at mid-day, and often our evening meal too. Tea-parties were a frequent occurrence, as people tried to maintain the social graces. We sat on stools, at a folding table, with our parents on folding canvas chairs, to escape the confined space of our cubicle. The same table served for card games, as Peter and I learnt rummy and whist. The mystery of trumps – what they were, and how lucky you were if your hand was full of them – all this I learnt in camp. Not in this case from our parents, but from Gwen Morris and Betty James, our adopted aunts, from the next-door cubicle in the church.

Lacking a study, my father would work outside in the good weather, preparing sermons, or material for his many classes. He took a folding chair to the shade of some bushes outside the church. The mahjong playing crowd set up tables on the grass outside the various houses, so the air would resound with the chink of ivory tiles. We made the most of the compound where we found ourselves.

Only a year ago Jean Irvine revisited the campus, with Fiona, a young relative; this was part of a visit to China which included Peking, Tientsin and Shanghai. They stayed in Yangchow in a high rise hotel, a mere three years old. Yangchow city appeared very clean to the travellers' eyes: its wide avenues decorated with flowers. There was no sign of spitting on the streets – a great contrast to the old China. Jean and Fiona made friends with the young hotel receptionist as they enquired about the former camp. The receptionist had good English but no-one of her generation knew anything of the war years, or had heard of Camp C. She agreed to accompany them and search out the compound. After one or two false alarms, that is, other campuses one of which was probably Yangchow A or B, the party located our compound, now used for training domestic science students. Among the ugly modern high-rise buildings, they found the former hospital, the Japanese commandant's house and the guardhouse. All were still standing, though the old grey brick buildings were in a derelict state. Jean and Fiona searched for the church, which they found only after asking its whereabouts from two present-day students:

> "Sure enough, away in a forlorn corner it stood, very sad and neglected, still standing but with no trees around, broken glass, very dilapidated and locked. Peered through the broken panes and it was just a shambles inside – still recognisable. I can't tell you how I felt and began to wonder if the past was all but a dream."

No-one questioned Jean and Fiona when they spent as long as possible the next morning at the compound. They were given free rein, after an initial check with the gatehouse guards, who gave permission to enter and take photographs. The gingko trees, protected by plaques bearing Chinese characters, remained from the war years. So too did the fir-tree under which Emma Hay and "Jumbo" Crank used to meet; they were later to marry. They made the most of their short time at Yangchow before leaving for Shanghai. Here they rediscovered Jean's old haunts, the Chartered Bank where her father had worked, and the remains of the Cathedral School. Jean and Fiona discovered the truth of L. P. Hartley's dictum:

> "The past is a foreign country; they do things differently there." [12]

[1] HFW, 17 October, 1945. See also Frances McAll, *The Moon Looks Down*, pp.46-7, for her initial impessions of Pootung.
[2] HFW, 29 April 1944
[3] For W. A. Macdonald's responsibility for camp garden, see the list of camp committees, date 9 April 1945. It survives among the camp's official papers, preserved by George Grant, our Camp Representative.
[4] HFW, 29 April 1945
[5] Brenda Henderson has her husband's collections; Neil Begley, pp.103-4
[6] Gilbert Manley, recollections, September 2002
[7] Neil Begley, p.104
[8] HFW, 19 July 1943
[9] Red Cross letter, from M. D. L. Wickings to S. E. F. Thorp, 29 June 1944, *penes* PRW
[10] For Hashizumi, see Gillison, *The Cross and the Dragon*, p.164
[11] HFW, 23 July 1944
[12] Letter from Jean Irvine to Marjorie Train, July 2002; L. P. Hartley, prologue to *The Go-Between*, 1953

Grace Harvey

Kitchen Team - Note the wooden kings for the vegetables.

68

Kitchen Shift – Team 'A'

The Back Field and Laundry. - Note the completed fortification on the rear wall, to the immediate right of the washing pole.

Yangchow Years

Queuing for a meal outside the dining-hall

Yangchow C Brownie Pack

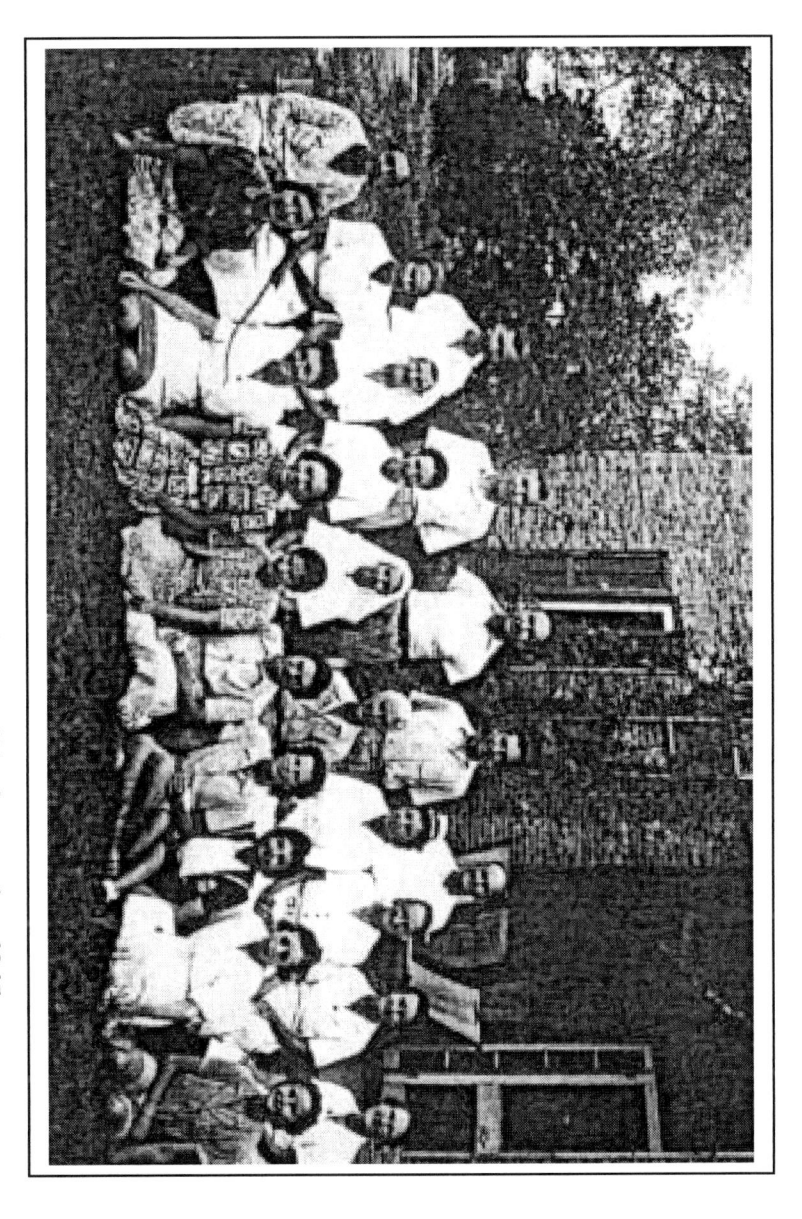

The camp medical and nursing staff in September 1945

American Hospital supply drop, of plaster-of-paris for Mrs Solomon's broken leg

No. 3 House, No. 4 House and Dining Room

The Dining Hall

Sample Text, as displayed in the camp dining hall, by G.C. Willis

The Bakery

The Church

The Hospital

Rear view of Hospital

The Gatehouse

The entrance to the Commandant's House

BIRTHS, MARRIAGE, DEATH

Births

Three babies were born during our time at Yangchow C: two were British, one Japanese. These were joyful occasions to offset the digging of graves in the small camp cemetery. The first to arrive was a baby son, Colin, born to the Taylor family, who already had a son and daughter of school age. [1]

The next child was Japanese. Tanaka, the father, was prominent among the guards. We internees found him harsh, since under his authority roll call was held outside in the snow:

> "Tanaka wanted us on parade, so we cut trenches in the snow for the lines to stand on." [2]

A week before this episode, Tanaka had gone off to get married. There had been a change over of some guards, because of a fight in February. Presumably Tanaka stayed until the child was born in the camp hospital:

> "Matron and Dr. Gell had to rush off while we sat and gossiped"

recorded Beryl, who was on hospital duty at this time. [3]

The final birth happened in the happy frenzy which followed the end of the war. Lilee Cook's child arrived in late August; the hospital staff visited the newborn baby the next day. This must have been the first child born to Lilee and her husband, as the camp list of children under 16 on 8 March 1944 gives none of that surname. Other women rallied round to provide a layette for Mrs. Cook and for one of the Belgian ladies:

"Lilee Cook and Mrs. Delabis are expecting babies. Mrs. Bennett is making baby clothes." [4]

Marriage

The only wedding celebrated at Yangchow was that of Nora Quincey and Robert "Bully" Bulldeath. The bride's talent for sport meant she coached the girls' softball teams: the Sparrows and Magpies, for instance. Bully, her fiancé, led the men's dorm to roll call each morning. He took enormous pride in his boots, which always shone with polish. His buddies, sworn bachelors from the infamous Hornets' Nest gave him a hard time for deserting them. Despising the marital state, they hung his bed outside the window of the bachelor dorm. For his wedding his sartorial elegance extended to a white suit, while Nora's ensemble was pink. The simple Catholic ceremony was celebrated by Father O'Collins on September 1st 1943, sanctioned by the Japanese commandant, and the camp committee. A storeroom was emptied and furnished to give the newlyweds sufficient privacy for their honeymoon. Of course the whole camp took a benevolent interest, especially the teenagers, pleased to see their softball coach enjoy a touch of romance. They used branches from the flowering shrubs in the compound to decorate the room for the reception. Then the young couple were left undisturbed in their small room. Inevitably the camp wags alluded to it as 'Honeymoon Lodge'. [5]

Death

Eight deaths occurred during our internment. The first, that of young John Rees, known as Sonny, was apparently due to constriction of the throat. Sonny, his mother's only child, had been an altar-boy, and was buried in altar-boy's robes. His last words were "Jesus, mercy", so Father O'Collins told those attending the Requiem Mass. His death made a deep impression, if only because it occurred so soon after we entered camp. My father expressed sympathy: "Very sad for widowed mother" while Beryl Piper noted:

"Poor Mrs. Rees. She just sits and looks at the children." [6]

Seven more deaths followed before we left Yangchow. Six were the deaths of adults aged 60 or over: all men, except one. Mr. Kale, Senior, was the first to die after John Rees. Then Mrs. Rogers, originally a transfer from Camp B, collapsed one hot, sticky Sunday in July 1944, from heart failure. Her husband was in the camp hospital, suffering from shingles at the time. People reported him as more distressed than they might have supposed. Mr. Ashdowne, a retired Harley Street surgeon, had been on holiday with his family in Shanghai during 1941. Mr. White died in September 1944, to be followed by A. J. Ross in January 1945, on a cold winter's night. My father conducted his funeral, just as he had done for old Mr. Kale. As Christian Scientists, Mrs. Kale and Jack, her son, had taken Mr. Kale's death with equanimity.

They were all buried in the cemetery, at the camp's south-west corner. Two people, from Camps A and B, also lay there: a certain G. M. Boyes (Camp A), who died in late August 1943, and A. Vitte (Camp B) whose death occurred less than a week after our camp received its last batch of people from Shanghai, in March 1943. [7]

The last death, of young Geoff Manley, seemed especially tragic. One of the VIth form, Geoff had drawn birthday cards for my parents' joint birthday. He also attended Mr. Willis' evangelical Bible class. According to Neil Begley, he became despondent, fearing he would never leave camp alive:

> "Attempts to break his depression were of no avail; within a week he was dead."

His death was peculiarly poignant, as it occurred in September 1945, after we had learnt of the Allied victory. Teddy Evans, Keith Martin and Colin Palmer dug his grave: young men mourning their friend. Keith bore the processional cross at Geoff's funeral. Matins the following Sunday included a memorial to him. "A good lad gone", wrote my father.[8]

---

[1] Beryl Piper, 12 September 1944
[2] Beryl Piper, 16 January 1945
[3] Beryl Piper, 27 March 1945
[4] Beryl Piper, 27 April 1945
[5] Angus, pp. 128-9 and Beryl Piper, 1 September 1943. For the Hornets' Nest material, Owen Manley, recollections
[6] Keith Martin, recollections, HFW, 22 June 1943 and Beryl Piper, 23 June 1943
[7] Keith Martin, recollections, June 2002. HFW diary passim. Rosemary Green's journal, 9 July 1944, for Mrs. Rogers' death. Details for those from Camps A and B, and plan of cemetery, from papers penes Mrs. Heather Sulerzyski, daughter of G. D. Grant, Camp Representative
[8] Keith Martin, letter to Walford Gillison, March 2001, and HFW entries for 4 and 9 September 1945. Neil Begley, p. 142. Chris Willis commented on Geoff's spiritual development in camp, Willis pp. 115-6

FATIGUES

> "The trivial round, the common task
> Would furnish all we ought to ask"
> John Keble

The word which occurs most often in my father's journal, during the first months of our internment, is "fatigues". By this he meant the routine jobs of stoking, cleaning, clearing and carrying, done by the men of the camp, in teams of eight. Further, the Japanese authorities required Yangchow C to bake bread for all three camps in the city, to dispose of our own garbage, and keep the drains in working order. There was also a good deal of shifting heaving loads – sometimes of materials, bricks, for instance, sometimes moving the heavy luggage of new arrivals, or of those changing billets within our camp. Occasional jobs: digging a new well, or digging the few graves needed during our two and a half years of internment – these fell to the men, too. At the outset, in March 1943 some buildings needed cleaning before they could be used, for instance cleaning the grates in the camp kitchen. [1]

Soon the regular jobs became routine, and receive no further mention. After the war ended, these jobs fell to Chinese coolies, the traditional source of labour in Chinese society, and among expatriate Westerners.

At the beginning, the task of making a roster of men to perform the routine jobs was one for Mr. Piper, together with my father. This was taxing, as many people gave both reasons and excuses for avoiding the unpleasant jobs. Some simply failed to turn up for duty; on one occasion only three men, out of the requisite eight, were actually present. [2]

Some men were obviously too old to manage the heavy jobs. In the first summer it was agreed that all men under 55 should take a turn at firing in the kitchen. This agreement followed a row over unsuitable fuel: a lot of brushwood had been cut for burning, but was found to be useless:

> "Fatigue-duty trying these days as brushwood cuts arms and legs, and is difficult to carry."

The heat of July in Central China made working conditions oppressive. Some stokers went on strike, so a camp meeting was called. It is easy to imagine the exasperation of men who had toiled in the heat to produce fuel, which was now declared unsuitable for its purpose. Two days later all meals were late, and disorganised too, because of the poor fuel.[3]

If age prevented some men from helping with the heavy jobs, others were in poor health. Some, like Ernie Hardman, had a chronic medical condition; his problem was cataract. Other men were temporarily out of action, with an attack of dysentery or malaria. Whatever the reason, anyone's absence from fatigue-duty placed a greater burden on those who were fit, and ready to undertake unpleasant chores such as distributing water, and stoking.

Stoking

Stoking in the main kitchen meant tending the fires in a bank of eight stoves, primitive affairs made of concrete. The stores held large cauldrons to boil all the water, for unboiled water was a health hazard, if one ventured to drink it. In these cauldrons, too, all our food was cooked. Stokers began their shift at 3:30 a.m. They started by fetching water from the storage kongs outside the kitchen. Heavy wooden buckets were used to carry the water. Once the cauldrons were full, fires were lit, and the water brought to the boil. All this had to be done before the arrival of the cooks, to prepare the breakfast congee.[4]

Sometimes the fuel was coal, often mainly coal-dust. Coal was provided when the authorities could obtain it. Alternatively, there was wood though, as we have seen, the brushwood cut to fuel the stoves was found to be quite unsuitable for this purpose. Sometimes trees had to be felled. When there was neither coal nor wood available, the stokers resorted to

> "huge hand-held bundles of reed, which were slowly fed into the grates. A difficult and dangerous task, with burns a common occurrence."

Reeds were also used to start fires when coal was available. Fay Angus reminds us that the reeds were gathered from the banks of the Grand Canal. Reeds were highly inflammable, so stokers risked burns; some of them were severe. Stokers worked one of two shifts, either the early one, or else an afternoon shift, in order to prepare our evening meals. Keith Martin thought:

> "the whole scene resembled Dante's Inferno" [5]

In time a club of young men, known as the Night Hawks, took over some of the stoking. They ranged in age from 14 or so to 17 years old. A lithe personable youth, nicknamed "Pee Wee" was their leader. Fay Westwood (now Fay Angus) as a teenager herself, took care to be friendly with the stokers. Her reward will have been an extra ration of hot water, or perhaps an extra odd munch on a carrot, filched from the kitchen. A good deal of muscle was involved in the task of cleansing the large cauldrons, always known by their Chinese name of Ko. According to Dr. Ralph Bolton, of the camp's medical team, a stoker occupied in carrying water had to shift a ton and a half, if the weight of bucket and the water it contained was counted. No wonder Hudson Felgate, who weighed 10 stone in March 1943 at the start of internment, lost weight. At our liberation in August 1945 he was 7 stone 12 pounds of muscle and bone. [6]

Night Patrol

Night patrol was the job of teams of two men. Their job was to prevent theft of stores from the kitchen, and to look out for hazards, particularly for fires. It was always important to check the food-store, when supplies were so short; anyone with inside knowledge of the kitchen might be tempted to purloin extra food, especially in the last few months of our internment. This was the reverse side of so many people's involvement in kitchen chores.

As for fire, on at least one occasion the incinerator was discovered smouldering, one night when Gordon Day and my father shared night patrol. Four buckets of water were needed to quench it, and the stokers' team had to be roused an hour before their usual time. Later on, as Rosemary Green's diary records, another fire, which began when a cauldron cover in the kitchen was burnt, had to be extinguished at 2 a.m. There were comprehensive arrangements to deal with fire: how it was to be extinguished, and how internees were to behave. Able-bodied men, equipped with buckets, were to report to J. L. Wade at the central well. Able-bodied women to report to Mrs. M. Willis at the Camp Fire Pole. Dr. Riddell and Mr. Dent were to take charge of the elderly and of children under 14, with their mothers, in the north-west corner of the camp. [7]

Drains

Caring for the drains was one of the most unpleasant chores. Jimmie Tomlin, a studious young man, was responsible for keeping the drains unblocked, during most of the camp's lifetime. It was a tough job, especially at the outset when some drains were completely blocked, and so were useless until the blockage was freed. Blockages caused most trouble at times of heavy rain. Jimmie could then be found unblocking them, and doing so without a grumble. In his odd spare moments, Jimmie would polish up his knowledge of French or Latin. [8]

Milking Fathers

Soya bean milk had been made for us children, when our family, together with other L.M.S. families were living in Hankow, before internment. Keith Gillison suggested at Yangchow that he, George Henderson and my father should grind soya beans, so the camp's children should have milk for breakfast. All three men had young children – the eldest was aged about eleven. The snag was that, like stoking, the job entailed an early start to the day, about 5:30 a.m. Initially there were teething troubles: the 'milking fathers' had to decide the best way to produce the soya bean milk. One of the keenest volunteers managed to make a hash of it; the result was a liquid remarkably akin to whitewash. Matters soon improved: we children soon had the strangely aromatic stuff to drink. It tasted faintly metallic. [9]

After one of his spells of fatigue duty was over, my father queried its value with the single word

"Worthwhile?"

He decided that it was valuable, for then some people could see that parsons were not afraid of dirty work. He hoped for the chance to take part in fatigues later on. And so he did, taking his turn at kitchen stoking, before teaching English and history in the camp school. [10]

Baking

How hot and enervating it was, to belong to one of the bakery teams! As a strong young man aged 18, Hudson Felgate found himself punching dough, in the first year at Yangchow C. Our bakery had to feed some thirteen hundred people, that is, all those in the three Yangchow camps. Initially, the bakers learnt their skills from some Chinese, but these soon departed. The Chinese brought in the original block of yeast which our bakers then had to keep going. The flour contained plenty of weevils, so the first task was to sift it, before mixing the bread dough.

With so many hungry mouths to feed, the bakery handled immense quantities of ingredients:

> "Each piece of dough you kneaded was about the size of a pillow; you did three or four of these each shift. Sweat poured off you, while you were 'punching dough'." [11]

Because the bakers worked a night shift, and the work was so hot, and consumed so much energy, the bakers succeeded in persuading the Japanese that they needed an extra night meal.

> "Rather foolishly they asked what we would like. Yangchow being the centre of a chicken and egg producing area, we asked, with tongue in cheek, for chicken and eggs. To our amazement a chicken and a few eggs appeared on the night shift, and for a short time we feasted ... The guards soon saw through this." [12]

Forming the dough into loaves was women's work. They cut off sections of dough, and threw them into the scales. Soon they became expert at guessing the exact weight. Last of all, the loaves were counted off, five to a tin, ready for the oven. On one occasion one of the kneaders incorporated too much air into her loaves. After the camp protested, a spot check was made on the raw loaves to discover the culprit. All the girls were suspect. Imagine Van Beynon's relief when the guilty party was found, and she, Van, was in the clear. Baking was not congenial, as far as Van was concerned.

Moving flour sacks was a two person job, because of their heavy weight. Sifting flour was the task girls hated most. Not only were they covered in flour from head to toe but also the complement of weevils revolted them. Early rising in the dark cold of winter, added to the arm-ache they developed from stretching around the large sieves, made the work

unpleasant. Van Beynon collapsed at the knees. It is not surprising that she preferred to practise her teaching skills on the younger children. [13]
Others felt differently, wanting to join a bakery team, with those who were their friends. Both Marjorie Train and Beryl Piper had been hospital orderlies; they told Matron Wheal that they wanted a change. She took their departure well. Soon they were kneading dough and receiving a small piece of sweet bread, as a perk. The perks were attached to kitchen duty – it was possible to slip an extra carrot into a pocket, to eat later, and made working there a coveted duty to some of the women. [14]

Kitchen Work

Women's work in the kitchen was, in one sense, lighter than the heavy manual work which fell to men. Most of the time, women were cutting up the vegetables which composed our mushy stew: carrots, yams, sweet potatoes and turnips among them. Often the vegetables were half rotten; they needed a good deal of chopping and paring if they were to be edible at all. Many women found that standing about, in the heat thrown out by the kitchen stoves, was extremely enervating, especially so when the temperature soared to 98° or 100°F in summer. Mondays were always difficult for our family, as Mum worked the afternoon shift, and so was not available to care for Peter and me, when school was over. And she was certainly not the only woman whose strength was sapped by long spells of kitchen duty. This is clear from the number of women who fainted at morning roll-call in summer-time. By May 1945, the kitchen rota had been completely reorganised so that a four-day roster was in operation. People worked in the morning on Day I, in the afternoon Day II; Days III and IV were holidays. [15]

Garbage Disposal

Garbage disposal was another unpleasant camp routine. It meant collecting all the rubbish from each accommodation block; then it was burnt in the incinerator, close to the camp's north-east corner. Henry

"Incinerator" Brown, as he was known, to distinguish him from others with the same surname, was in charge of the incineration for most of our internment. Latterly, though, he gave up this job, and Chris Willis was asked to take over from the six-man team which had helped Mr. Brown. Willis agreed and, with Jimmie Tomlin as aide, managed to get rid of a plague of bluebottles. The flies were dispersed by Willis and Tomlin sprinkling lime wherever the bluebottles were thickest. Jean Willis, writing after our "liberation" while we were all still in camp, thought the outdoor work of cleaning up the garbage suited her husband's health. But it was not an easy task as "so many of the men are slackers". [16]

Public Works

The Public Works – or Maintenance – Department led by Mr. Savage had oversight of garbage disposal, as well as dealing with a host of other minor problems; the reed matting which divided cubicles from one another needed repair periodically. Our own matting was greatly improved by the P.W.D. team. Savage looked after the routine maintenance in an exemplary fashion. [17]

Most heavy tasks fell, inevitably, to the able-bodied men. A good example is the work in the dining-hall which was used for many things, starting with early Mass, and later, for our school. This involved much furniture shifting. Jobs like shifting heavy iron stoves about showed up the difference between those who worked hard, and others who took every chance to down tools, and knock off; my father's irritation comes across in his comment:

"Fed up with those who did little." [18]

Nurses and Orderlies

Matron Wheal and Nurse Alice Jagger were the full-time nursing staff of the hospital. Jags, as Miss Jagger was called by everyone, ran a regular clinic each day for small ailments: cuts and bruises, mosquito bites which turned septic, anything which needed a splash of gentian violet or a bandage. Besides these two full-time nurses, other part-time nurses staffed the wards. We were fortunate to have Mrs. Jewell, aunt to Keith Martin and mother to Peter, Mrs. Edwina Longhurst, and Miss Hilda Shepherd, from the L.M.S. All were professionally qualified. They had teenage girl orderlies to help them: the Main sisters, Margery and Joan, and Beryl Piper were among the orderlies. Beryl made friends with Gwen Morris, the L.M.S. missionary, who was often in severe pain with attacks of sciatica, and so was treated in hospital. Gwen was a cheerful person, with the curly hair and dark skin which makes her so easy to pick out from camp photos. When not in hospital, she taught Mandarin Chinese to anyone who wished to learn. Despite the age-gap between them, Beryl in her mid-teens and Gwen in her thirties found each other good company. Even missionaries could enjoy a game of bridge, as Beryl discovered. Not all orderlies were girls; Colin Palmer, intent on a medical career, served as orderly and surgical assistant after School Certificate exams in July 1944.[19]

One of the best places to work was the small hospital kitchen which produced special diets. These were intended for the sick, or frail elderly people, who might be confined to their own accommodation, as well as for those actually in hospital. Mrs. Goodman, Zena's mother, was one of the mainstays of the hospital kitchen. Zena's diary details some of this work. When this work was over, Mrs. Goodman sometimes produced goodies for special occasions among her own circle, especially when ingredients from the Red Cross parcels were available. Zena will have learnt to cook alongside her mother in the hospital kitchen. A hospital diet was not only provided for in-patients but also for certain out-patients, but only if they had a doctor's recommendation. Often the food was bland, using some of the goats' milk. Colin Palmer recalls collecting portions of hospital food for his mother, whose weight had dropped as low as 6 stone in camp.[20]

The able bodied men of the camp carried an enormous burden. Before Pearl Harbour in December 1941 and the outbreak of the Pacific War, many young men had left Shanghai to join the British armed forces. So there was a shortage of men in the 20 – 40 year age-group. Hence the ratio of men to women - 208 men to 304 women - was such that the younger men, those aged 16 and over, had to do many of the heavy tasks. There was always luggage to shift, or piles of heavy bedding to move, whenever people moved from one billet to another. Hence teenage muscle was in demand, even though the young men were still at school. Moreover many older men were either too old or too lazy to undertake heavy work. Teenagers like Teddy Evans, Ray Azachee, Keith Martin and Colin Palmer knew they had to get good marks at school, so they could make something of their future. Life was challenging for these students, so well-known to my father, as he taught them. Vanny Beynon's sister Joan was academically gifted, and a rival to Keith for first place in the VI form. When she was 9 marks ahead, at the end of the summer, my father, loyal to his sex, wrote:

> "All the boys have done hard labour tasks (well-digging etc.) while she, Joan, had leisure to swot in the afternoons." [21]

Since a commission was appointed to consider camp labour, about halfway through our time at Yangchow, I conclude that some men must have protested that others were evading their fatigue duties. The commission's report ended with the words:

> "It strongly recommends that no schoolboy should be permitted to stoke."

So able-bodied adults like George Green did their five-hour shifts of stoking, while the strength of the sixteen and seventeen year old lads was not unduly exploited. [22]

Without people doing routine duties, often unpleasant and always tiring, the camp's organisation would have collapsed. It is a tribute to "Skipper" Grant and to the camp committee that the jobs were done right up to September 1945. Then Chinese cooks and coolies took over. "Simmy" – J. L. Simmons - arranged this through Chinese pastors from Yangchow town. They organised an influx of amahs and coolies; in return the pastors asked my father to help them recover their church property from the Japanese and the puppet Chinese military. The changeover of camp routines was swiftly effected; within three days the Chinese had taken over the routines of cooking and cleansing. As for the church property, I do not know whether it was ever recovered, or if it was, in what kind of condition it had survived. [23]

It is clear that many people did their tasks faithfully, without undue complaint. Cheerfulness did break in as people established a camaraderie of team work. They followed the guidelines framed by the camp's labour committee. A few people manufactured excuses, evaded their responsibilities, preferring to spend their afternoons playing bridge or mahjong. Peggy Taylor gives us a picture of four elderly men

> "excused from the work force because of age and infirmity. They spent their days playing Contract Bridge – they were seasoned players but rarely in agreement about each other's bidding or play, the arguments becoming quite heated. They sat under a tree when the weather was right and were a great source of entertainment for the passing parade." [24]

1. HFW, 20 March 1943
2. HFW, 23 and 24 March 1943
3. HFW, 13 July 1943
4. Hudson Felgate, unpublished memoir p.10
5. Peggy Taylor, unpublished memoir, p.6; Angus, *White Pagoda*, pp.118 and 120. Also Keith Martin, unpublished memoir, p.13
6. Angus, *White Pagoda*, p.120. Keith Martin, unpublished memoir, p.13 and Hudson Felgate, also unpublished memoir, p.13
7. For night patrol, see HFW passim. For the cauldron incident, see Rosemary Green, 27 March 1944. Also fire regulations issued by camp committee, 27 April 1945.
8. Willis, p.97, and Walford Gillison, recollections, June 2002
9. HFW, 26 May 1943
10. HFW, 31 March and 18 August 1943
11. Hudson Felgate, unpublished memoir, p.7
12. Hudson Felgate, unpublished memoir, p.7
13. Myfanwy Beynon, recollections, February 2003, and Peggy Taylor, unpublished memoir, p.6
14. Beryl Piper, 24 and 29 July 1945; also Angus, p.118
15. Rosemary Green, 17 May 1945
16. Willis, pp.126-7, and Jean Willis, letter to relatives in Canada, 10 September 1945
17. HFW, 20 November 1943, and Willis, p.98
18. HFW, 6 April 1943
19. Beryl Piper, passim and C.A.L. Palmer, recollections, October 2002
20. Zena Goodman, passim, and C. A .L. Palmer, recollections, September 2002
21. HFW, 30 June 1945
22. Report and recommendations of commission appointed to consider camp labour, c. 27 July 1944 and Rosemary Green, 27 March 1944
23. HFW, 10-13 September 1945
24. Peggy Taylor, unpublished memoir, p.9

PEOPLE

"All sorts and conditions of men"
Book of Common Prayer

The questions most people ask about internment are: How many people were there at Yangchow? Were you all British, or were there others, too? What kind of people were they? How well did you get on together?

A brief reply would run:

There were, roughly, some 610 of us, from most parts of what was then the British Empire, together with 38 Belgians, who joined us part-way through. We came from many differing professions and occupations. There was a certain amount of tension between different groups, and also between individuals. Sometimes this was creative tension, in that new patterns of organisation might develop, as with the various fatigues. Eventually we all shook down together, in the great kaleidoscope of wartime.

But this is only an outline; there was rather more to it than that.

Between 600 and 650 people: men, women and children were interned in Yangchow C in the last two and a half years of the war. The actual number fluctuated a good deal as people came and went, first, between the three Yangchow camps, and later on, between Yangchow C and Shanghai. In this case, individuals were occasionally allowed downriver, for medical treatment in Shanghai.

In late September 1943, there was a general post: most of those from camps A and B left Yangchow, and were fitted into some of the

Yangchow Years

Shanghai camps – Pootung and Lunghua for instance. This rearrangement was made possible because some Americans were repatriated in August 1943; naturally there were rumours that we, in camp C, might well be moved, too. Among those who left our camp was a Salvation Army family: the wife and younger children of Major George Walker. He himself was in Haiphong Rd., that notorious Shanghai camp for professional men, for senior business men, for some employees of the Shanghai Municipal Council, and police officers.

> "Mrs. Walker, Joan and Howard off to A camp, preparatory to going to Shanghai ... some A and B people brought here in exchange – a mix-up." [1]

Angus Mackinnon and his wife were another two who had begun internment at Yangchow C. In the summer of 1943, their friends were very concerned for Mackinnon's health; they feared he had bowel cancer. The outlook then was bleak: "he might as well stay here among friends", suggested some of them. However, after a farewell party, the Mackinnons left for Shanghai:

> "Mackinnons away at 6:30 ... for his operation for cancer. Shall we ever see him again?"

Young Ian Mackinnon stayed at Yangchow for almost all the rest of the war. He was officially in the care of my father; he went to the camp school, became an assistant goatherd, and lived for some time with the Goodman family, as he was of an age with John Goodman. Eventually Ian was transferred to Lunghua; it was easier for him to visit his father in hospital from here. Ian was in Lunghua from May 1945 until the camp was liberated. [2]

Another person who left Yangchow C early on was Mrs. Josephine Willson. Her name appears among the many signatures which accompany the pencil sketch of House 2, drawn by Rosemary Green in her autograph book. My father's diary records his talking with Mrs.

Willson on a few occasions; not surprising when we realise she had lost her husband who had died in the notorious Haiphong Rd. camp. The widow, together with one or two others, left Yangchow in early October, in the care of Dr. 'David' Gell. Dr. Gell herself returned soon after; probably Mrs. Willson and the others went into another of the Shanghai camps, after medical treatment. [3]

It is tedious to quote further examples; suffice to state that the total number of people under Commandant Hashizumi's authority was never constant for more than a few weeks. The largest influx was the advent of 38 Belgian men, women and children in mid-November 1944.

By the time all the main groups had reached Yangchow C in mid-March 1943 there were 621 people in camp, according to my father. Mr. Myerscough with a recently broken kneecap had already been taken to Chinkiang hospital; his wife will have accompanied him as Fred Myerscough was blind, and depended on her guidance. They returned within the month. Among those arriving later was Father Thornton, in June 1943. And in early November 1944, we were joined by young de Rago; he came from Shanghai to join his father and cousins at Yangchow, just before the Belgians arrived. [4]

An apparently definitive list of those in camp on 8 March 1944 gives a total of 610 people. Of these, 304 were women, 208 men, with 98 children, of whom 52 were boys, and 46 girls. With the Belgians - 16 men, 11 women, and 11 children, 6 boys and 5 girls - this makes a total of 648 people, the maximum of those interned at Yangchow C in November 1944. [5]

Our camp boasted a fine diversity of occupations among its adult population, drawn from the foreigners of Shanghai. Clerics, doctors, nurses, engineers, owners of small businesses, taipans accustomed to command, and clerks used to obedience were all present in the microcosm which was Yangchow C. The perennial rivalry between the seekers of souls and the seekers of profit, to borrow a phrase from Desmond Power, was much in evidence. [6]

Accountancy was represented by Ernie Hardman and Cecil Longhurst. One of the doctors was a general practitioner from Shanghai – Rob Symons. The other three – "David" Gell, Keith Gillison and Ralph Bolton – were all missionaries. So, too, were Hilda Shepherd, Alice Jagger and Matron Wheal, while married women – Edwina Longhurst and "Brownie" Jewell – were also trained nurses. Dr. Riddell was dentist to all three Yangchow camps, until the A and B camp people returned to Shanghai.

Mrs. Corneck had run a secretarial college before internment; Mrs. Ruby Taylor, owner of the Peter Pan International School for young children, in the Rue Boissezon, in the French Concession of Shanghai, lost all the contents of her school when the Japanese Imperial army took over the school and everything in it, in March 1943. The business world was well represented: Wattie Brown had previously been the secretary of the Shanghai Gas Company. Duncan Main had owned a food-processing business. He was an old China hand, as the son of Dr. David Main, a C.M.S. missionary doctor from Scotland. [7]

Captain McIlwain was a retired sea-captain, an old salt, who sported a homburg hat a good deal of the time. Flo, his wife was nearly 30 years younger than he. His favourite smoke was Navy Cut tobacco; too often in camp he had to make do with tea-leaves.

Alec Glass and Frank Mulvey were both engineers, whose expertise was to prove valuable for us. Mr. Philips, father of Irene and Reg, was a shipyard engineer. One of the Messrs. Taylor kept a philatelist's shop in Shanghai. A younger Mr. William Taylor was one of three people who worked for Asiatic Petroleum Co. (Shell); the others were Arthur Piper, father to Beryl, of the diary, and Walter Palmer, whose son Colin was one of the stars of the camp's VIth form. As for Lewis P. Quincey, he had run a gymnasium in 'Shanghai days; a fluent Chinese speaker, he was not tall, but stocky in build, 'hail fellow well met' in manner, and brown as a berry to look at. Truly we were a mixed bunch.

As for the clergy, Father O'Collins and Father Jim Thornton were the two Catholic priests, while Revd. P. C. Matthews was the only ordained Anglican. He wore "two hats" – that is, he also acted as headmaster of the Yangchow Boys' School. Both PCM, as we knew him, and my father had been selected by the B.R.A. to act as chaplains, PCM for the Anglicans, and my father, ably supported by Revd. George Henderson for the Free Church community. Major Colin Begley and Edith, his wife, were experienced Salvation Army missionaries from Australia; they had been interned previously in Stanley camp, Hong Kong. Major Begley was to work alongside Sir Cyril Young, an Irish baronet. He and his family came the closest to what we might term 'aristocracy'.

Some of the camp's women were full-time wives and mothers; others like Mrs. Westwood, mother to Fay, had been employed in Shanghai; she had been an accountant at the well-known shipping firm of Butterfield & Swire. Three of the L.M.S. women were teachers: Betty James and Gwen Morris, her great friend and colleague, as well as Kath Gillison, the wife of Keith Gillison, the camp surgeon. Joan Penfold, soon to become head of the girls' school, persuaded all three to become teachers at Yangchow. Miss Penfold also secured Maida Morton-Smith to teach languages; Helen Willis, sister to Chris, knew enough Greek to plan a translation of the New Testament, but Joan Penfold was persuasive enough to secure Miss Willis, too, as a teacher; in so doing, she became a close friend of the Willis family. [8]

Many of these people were missionaries from the United Kingdom, Australia or Canada. The missionaries overlap with the professional groups, most obviously in the case of the medics.

In age we ranged from kindergarten children to people well over 70. Mona Nissim, a month my senior, and I were among the youngest; we were 5 at the outset, and nearly 8 at liberation. Colin Taylor, born in

September 1944, had the distinction of being the only camp baby, until the last months of the war. There were three young children – two in the Barbe family and one in the Delabies, among the Belgians who came in November 1944.

At the other end of the spectrum a number of people were 74 or older, when we left camp. Walter Milward (79), cared for by the Hendersons, was among them; so too were the parents of Joan Penfold: Fred (74) and Mrs. Susan Penfold (77). The well-known botanical expert, Dr. Chadwick Kew, of the Shanghai British Nursery was, at 74, just younger than Captain McIlwain. By a strange coincidence both men had wives called "Flo" or "Florence" some twenty years, or more, younger than their husbands. The elderly ladies included Mrs. Nissim, grandmother to the two Nissim families. None of the Belgians was over 70 – Pierre Vissers (68) and Charles Biron (60) were the most senior. [9]

We should note that the camp's age-profile was skewed with a high proportion of children, of women and of men over the age of 45. There were comparatively few men in the 20-40 age group. This was characteristic of internment camps in China in the Shanghai area, in contrast to camps in Malaya, Singapore and Hong Kong, where there were more men of all ages. [10]

Racially we were a mixed bunch; in this respect Yangchow C was similar to other civilian camps in China. The British included people from the entire United Kingdom, with Scots like Betty James, from Glasgow, and the Beynon family, from Wales. Those with British passports included White Russians, mostly women and children, such as Mrs. Anna Nicholls, who had her daughter and teenage son, Reg, with her. The White Russians had left their homeland at, or soon after, the 1917 revolution. Many of those in Yangchow C had married British servicemen. A good example is Mrs. Olga Linkhorn, with her son Michael. Olga had married a seaman, A. B. Linkhorn; he was one of those killed when the Japanese sank H.M.S. Peterel in December 1941. [11]

Olga Linkhorn was one of the so-called "loose women" – a delightfully unfortunate term used by the Japanese, to describe women with no attendant male: spinsters, widows or those whose husbands were elsewhere.

Eurasians were interned, too, if they held British passports. At the assembly in Shanghai Cathedral, Fay Westwood recalls:

> "Eurasian girls of exceptional beauty, with black Chinese hair, slender oriental bodies, and the fair-skinned, blue-eyed English characteristics."

Eurasians were often regarded with hostility by some English folk from conventional backgrounds who stigmatised Eurasians as pleasure-seeking and indolent. But Mary Lou Newman, in her teens in Yangchow days, was impressed by the great kindliness, and positive attitude to hard work of the Eurasians she met then. To Hudson Felgate, both the Russians and Eurasians were

> " ... marvellous. They were proud and grateful for being British, and they worked very hard. But that's to be expected, as they all had a hard job to get their British passports." [12]

The Jewish community comprised some fifty adults, with nine children. Many were Sephardic Jews, descendants of those expelled from Spain by Ferdinand and Isabella, in 1492. They had reached the Far East via North Africa, the Ottoman empire, and India. A good example is the large Nissim clan – eleven people all together. The Nissims included two sons, with their wives and families, together with the sons' elderly mother. [13]

Finally, there were sixteen Canadians, notably the Day family of four, and Chris Willis, with his wife, Jean, and sister, Helen. At least two people had American citizenship: Mrs. Marco, and Father James

Thornton, though the latter was of Irish stock. Mrs. June Hall was American by birth, but married to an Englishman. [14]

> "The pukka white Brit who was used to the lazy life in the Far East … with plenty of servants, did not show up too well in camp."

Hudson Felgate is by no means the only critic of the Shanghai taipans. Chris Willis, writing soon after the war ended, mentions:

> "a number not in love with labour"

After describing the justification given by one of the "slackers", Willis continued:

> "by far the heaviest end of the work fell on a comparatively few who were willing to do it."

Willis felt that this was a mistake, as the hardworking carried an undue burden. My father shared Willis' opinion; long after we had left Yangchow, he wrote:

> "Some folk were very kind; they did good work and did not grumble."

By implication, others did not; naming no names, he was critical of those who lacked what he saw as a moral sense, and whose views on religious matters were "hazy". His diary has occasional references to individuals who evaded the tasks assigned to them. Keith Gillison made the same point in a different way:

> "Camp contained all sorts, from the constantly miserable to the irrepressibly happy. There were those primarily out for themselves, and those doing all they could to help others." [15]

An interesting example of independence is to be found in the position adopted by Albert Nissim's father, Nooriel. He had been a successful realtor in Shanghai, before camp, working in partnership with his brother, Marcus. Albert stresses his father's wish to preserve his independence at Yangchow:

> "He did not want to be regimented into kitchen or other duties, so he took it upon himself to clean and maintain all the drains ... a very dirty job, but one he did alone and he worked very hard at this."

Nooriel Nissim also served on the camp committee for much of the period in camp, and took those responsibilities very seriously as well. Nazira, his wife, worked both in the camp hospital and in the kitchen, as well as supervising some of the activities of the girls since Rachelle and Mona, her daughters, were among the young girls in camp. [16]

In fairness to the taipans, we should recall that their Shanghai lifestyle depended on Chinese labour. Some of them never adjusted to the fatigues essential to the smooth running of the camp, while others took on their new and very different responsibilities with relative ease, and co-operated in the schedules issued by the Labour committee.

Our tiny world of over 600 individuals bore out the truth of the old Yorkshire saying:

"There's nowt so queer as folk."

Put in another fashion, we all had to meet

> "the challenge of living with others of very different social backgrounds, under similar conditions of privation and captivity."

Keith Martin expressed this well. He continued:

> "In those three years ideas were changed, some tolerance of other customs and beliefs developed."

Probably those of us aged ten and under found life easiest, since we had little normal life with which we could compare Yangchow conditions. [17]

---

1. HFW, 29 September 1943. For Haiphong Rd., see Hugh Collar, *Captive in Shanghai*; Norman Cliff's book, *Prisoners of the Samurai*, gives further detail on George Walker, pp.49–52.
2. HFW, 14, 25 and 26 July 1943, and Ian Mackinnon, recollections, November 2002.
3. HFW, 23 June and 12 October 1943.
4. HFW, 1 April 1943. For the Myerscough's departure and return, HFW, 20 March and 9 April 1943. For Father Thornton, HFW, 12 June 1943. For de Rago, see Beryl Piper, 2 November 1944.
5. Camp list as at 8 March 1944. This typed list has the names of the Belgians added in longhand.
6. Desmond Power, *Little Foreign Devil*, p.205/6.
7. Peggy Taylor, unpublished memoir, pp.2-3. Information on Mrs. Corneck from Keith Martin, also Beryl Piper, passim. For Dr. David Main, see S. D. Sturton, *From Mission Hospital to Concentration Camp*, p.18.
8. Angus, p.21; Gillison, p.160; Willis, p.108.
9. All the ages are quoted from the camp list of those remaining at Yangchow C on 27 September 1945.
10. I owe this point to the insights of Keith Martin and Ron Bridge.
11. For A. B. Linkhorn, see Hugh Collar, *Captive in Shanghai*, p.16.
12. Angus, p.105; Mary Lou Newman, recollections, September 2002 and Hudson Felgate, unpublished memoir, p.5.
13. For the Nissims, see Albert Nissim, recollections, December 2002.
14. Canadian nationals from a list among G. D. Grant's papers; the Americans from the list dated 27 September 1945.
15. Hudson Felgate, unpublished memoir, p.5; Willis, p.69; HFW, brief notes written, Gillison, p.164
16. Albert Nissim, recollections, December 2002
17. Keith Martin, memoir, November 2002

HEALTH

> "Look to your health, and if you have it, praise God, and value it next to a good conscience, for health is the second blessing that we mortals are capable of."
> Isaac Walton, *Compleat Angler*

In its original decisions over the deployment of qualified personnel to the various internment camps, the B.R.A. chose four doctors for Yangchow C : Keith Gillison, an LMS missionary, of the Union Hospital, Hankow; Ralph Bolton, of the Methodist Missionary Society, experienced both as a physician, surgeon and ophthalmologist. Dr. Mary Gell, the lady doctor from the S.P.G. was nicknamed 'David', though why I do not know. Dr. Rob Symons came from general practice in Shanghai. Yangchow C also had a dentist: Dr. J. D. Riddell. Two nurses, Miss Wheal and Miss Jagger, were fully qualified and B.M.S. missionaries. The latter was always called 'Jags'. We were also fortunate in having other qualified nursing staff: Mrs. Jewell, for instance, was S.R.C.N. (State Registered Children's Nurse). She worked part-time in the hospital. So too did Mrs. Edwina Longhurst, stepmother to Patsy Longhurst. She was also a nursing sister.

While Yangchow Camps A and B still existed, there was considerable co-operation between all three, in terms of medical care. Internees from A or B came to C, for Mr. Riddell's attention. His dentistry was organised from an office in the camp hospital. Riddell could not bring the electrical equipment which provided power for his drills with him. Probably it was lost in transit. Keith Gillison describes the ingenuity that went into filling a cavity in one of his own teeth. Riddell's drill worked in conjunction with one of the camp's carpentry team:

"The carpenter supplied the power, the dentist his expertise." [1] However, the carpenters were dissatisfied. Working with camp mechanics, they manufactured a wheel and treadle, akin to a spinning-wheel. They used some expanding curtain wire which Gillison had brought with him into camp; this transmitted the rotation from the spinning wheel to the drill. Riddell's technology was so improved that he could dispense with the services of an assistant. [2]

Since we lacked sweets in camp, except for occasional treats of peanut brittle from the canteen, or equally occasional chocolate from the parcels we received, it may be that deprivation was good for our teeth.

People with dental plates sometimes found themselves in difficulty if a plate broke. W. G. Bown, one of the internees, had a small workshop adjacent to the hospital where he repaired watches, or other possessions. With the metal working tools he had previously used for recreation, he succeeded in making a new plate for someone who had broken hers. Bown persuaded Dr. Riddell to take a plaster-of-paris impression of her mouth. Then he beat out a silver shilling until it fitted the mould exactly. He removed the teeth from the old, broken plate:

> "He prepared little strips of silver, and soldered each tooth to the frame he had made. The new plate fitted better, and worked better than anything she had ever had before." [3]

No wonder the workshop was besieged with requests for repairs to other dental plates, once the word got around the camp.

Ear, nose and throat cases were the speciality of Dr. Gale, another L.M.S. surgeon from one of the other Yangchow camps. He came to camp C to deal with a mastoid case, a girl suffering from a severe infection. Keith Gillison details the full story in his book; suffice to say, a special ENT instrument was made, to use in the mastoid case. The instrument was a self-retaining retractor, used to hold skin and subcutaneous tissue away from the infected bone. One of the children loaned some perforated strips from a Meccano set, together with the necessary nuts and bolts:

> "Two metal strips were cut from an empty tin ... and a St. Andrew's Cross-shaped tool, hinged at the middle, was made ... The retractor, together with some carpentry chisels and gouges, and the instruments routinely used, were boiled up, and proved very satisfactory. The patient did well." [4]

The standard of medical care was high. Apart from the hospital, there was also a clinic, which dealt with such minor ailments as prickly heat in summer, infected mosquito bites, anointed with copious use of gentian violet, and also with any minor burns which afflicted the young men who scalded themselves with boiling water from the hot-water shop. Gentian violet again was the only remedy available for these burns. [5] In winter most people suffered from chilblains; they afflicted most of those whose memories of Yangchow I have tapped. Beryl Piper kept to her bed during the severe weather of January 1945, hoping her chilblains would improve. Later, Beryl herself treated Mona Nissim, one of the young Jewish girls:

> "Poor little Mona has chilblains on her feet." [6]

Both Fay Westwood and my father had chilblains, too. My father blamed the deficiencies in our diet, as well as the low temperatures.

> "[Our ears] became red, itched and burned ... the skin split and burst ... the pain was excruciating." [7]

The younger boys rubbed their chilblains with snow, but this only exacerbated the problem. Gilbert Manley's fingers were affected so severely that they are distorted to this day.

> "First grossly swollen, like red and white bananas, shiny ... itching so badly especially in sunshine or near any source of warmth ... Having to ask someone to undo my fly-buttons. Oh, the shame of it!" [8]

Prickly heat in summer seemed particularly virulent on parts of the body subject to pressure from clothes: round the waist, for instance, so that the waistband of skirt or trousers irritated the skin condition. Sunstroke too was dangerous. Just standing on parade for roll-call for 20 minutes, in the extreme heat - temperatures were frequently over 100°F – caused the more fragile women to faint. Many of the surviving photos show youngsters wearing cotton hats in summer, to prevent sunstroke. I myself caught sunstroke, probably by forgetting my sunhat. I was delirious; my parents summoned Dr. Gell at 3 a.m. because of my high fever. I was still unwell at the start of the new school term. [9]

Medical staff appointed to Yangchow C used the weeks prior to entry in March 1943 to prepare their medicines and other equipment. The hospital intended for all these Yangchow camps, was soon set up in House no. 1. Outpatients were treated downstairs; a maximum of 14 inpatients upstairs. There was no electricity; the operating table was placed beneath a skylight in the single-storey kitchen. Surgical instruments, together with gloves and other requirements, were sterilised in one of the vast cauldrons, normally used for cooking. The surgeons – Keith Gillison and Ralph Bolton – had ensured they had materials for anaesthesia, too. After the initial medical examination provided for all internees a mastectomy was judged necessary for one of the ladies.

Appendicitis afflicted both campers and one of the Japanese. When Peter Jewell, then aged 11, was having his appendix removed, his mother, a part-time sister, overheard the surgeon's comment:

> "I had not realised how thin our children had grown."

One of the guards also needed an appendectomy. The medics used this opportunity to demand more drugs from the Japanese authorities. The surgery was conducted at gunpoint, but all went well, despite the audience of guards. [10]

One of the teenage girls, Beryl Smith, also had her appendix removed by Keith Gillison, assisted by Dr. Rob Symons, while Matron Wheal administered the anaesthetic. Young Beryl Piper, then a hospital orderly, was asked if she would like to watch and she accepted. [11]

Sometimes surgeons operated in the patient's own room: Mrs. Leys, one of the Belgians, had a boil on her leg; Dr. Gillison aided by Nurse Jagger, lanced it, using a local anaesthetic. [12]

Again, Colin Palmer's own father, W. A. L. Palmer needed surgery of a minor variety; Dr. Gillison operated, while Dr. Bolton gave the anaesthetic. As a would-be medical student, Colin himself was allowed to watch. [13]

Billy Spencer's story shows how successful the camp's surgeons could be. At the outset of camp, Billy – a lad in his mid-teens – could only walk with the help of two sticks, because of his deformed legs. He "walked" on the sides of his feet. His disability cut him off from the active games of the other lads; he kept cheerful, despite his becoming a loner. A retired Harley Street surgeon, elderly Mr. Ashdowne, uncle to Michael and Hilary in the camp school, was only in Yangchow because he had been visiting his relatives in Shanghai in March 1943. He felt too old to do the surgery himself, but acted as adviser and consultant to Drs. Bolton and Gillison. Colin Palmer suggests that Billy had had a birth defect: a tendon which needed lengthening. After the operation, Billy took regular exercise, and was then able to walk normally, so could join his friends' games. It may be that his parents did not know, prior to camp, that surgery was possible; maybe they could not have afforded it, even if they had known. Yangchow and its surgeons transformed Billy's life; he and his parents may have been some of the few who thanked Providence for internment. [14]

Not all medical care took place within the camp. Blind Mr. Myerscough, who depended on his wife's attendance, was treated for a broken kneecap in the Chinkiang hospital. After two and a half weeks he returned to the camp hospital. [15] A more serious case was that of Angus Mackinnnon, diagnosed with cancer. He and his wife left Yangchow for Shanghai; Ian, their son, was left to my father's care.

> "Mackinnons away at 6.30 … Shall we ever see him again? Ian in my care, a responsibility." [16]

Even as late as May 1945 the authorities allowed a few people to go to Shanghai for medical treatment: two of the Jewish Moses family, and Mr. Lamb; the latter needed dental care. On the return of this small group, they brought welcome news of Shanghai: the "tremendous food prices – one cake cost $6,000, the armed guards, the seething atmosphere of tension." But one criticism made of Hashizumi in 1947 was that Mrs. Rees was forbidden to visit Shanghai, for surgery. [17]

Owen Beynon, the Welsh pharmacist, was another significant person in the camp's medical team; like Gillison and my father he was an L.M.S. missionary. He appears in the photograph of the hospital staff, in September 1945. Fiery Mr. Beynon, of short stature, is in the back row with the doctors, while the professional nursing staff grace the middle row. A bevy of girls acted as orderlies. They included Marjorie Train, Beryl Piper and Joan Main. Joan intended to pursue a nursing career. The Imperial War Museum preserves a letter of recommendation for Joan, written by Matron Alice Wheal, herself trained at St. Bartholomew's in London. The letter to St. Bartholomew's nursing school details Joan's varied hospital experience as orderly and nursing assistant at Yangchow. [18]

Returning to Mr. Beynon, he was in charge of the X-ray equipment. Early on in our internment, I recollect his showing my parents the plates of the X-rays of my brother's and my own chests; this was in March 1943. Two years later, Peter's chest X-ray showed he had had pleurisy, following a severe bout of broncho-pneumonia, lasting five weeks. [19]

The two most common scourges at Yangchow were malaria and dysentery. Recurrent attacks of malaria were common; my own mother suffered from it. Young Neil Begley, son of the Salvation Army's Major Begley, was sent home from class by Father Thornton. Neil shook uncontrollably, so that Ian, his brother, had to sit on his bed, to stop it rattling. In his delirium, Neil's temperature reached 107°F. Lacking appropriate drugs, the nurses could only fan him, and sponge him with cold water. The fever abated, but recurred the next day. Neil could predict the onset of malaria: 2.45 p.m. every second Friday. Others were equally predictable: Muriel Millar, for instance. [20]

Neil's classmate Walford, son of the camp surgeon, endured recurrent malaria too. After the U.S. officers brought medicines in September 1945, Walford was given atabrine as a prophylactic. Atabrine turns the skin yellow. "Chinky" Gillison became Walford's inevitable nickname later on at Eltham College, the public school originally founded to educate the sons of overseas missionaries. [21]

Mrs. Beynon, wife to Owen Beynon, the pharmacist, was frequently in hospital with malaria, as Zena Goodman's diary attests. For this reason, the entire Beynon family was one of the first to leave camp in September 1945. Later on, my father visited Mrs. Beynon, in the Lester Hospital, Shanghai, where she was recovering from malaria and pneumonia. [22]

Dysentery was endemic, probably owing to defective sanitation and polluted water supplies. Dysentery cases often filled the hospital wards. Owen Beynon himself was seriously ill with the bacillary form in July 1943. A mini-epidemic of amoebic dysentery afflicted the camp at the end of the war. We were fortunate that the American medics who arrived in early September 1945 brought a new drug – emetine – which was very effective. [23]

A number of factors contributed towards the fair physical condition of most Yangchow internees at the end of the war. First the excellent care of nurses, doctors and hospital orderlies. Living in such close proximity to each other, doctors were not remote figures, only to be approached with trepidation. They took a full part in the camp's social life. Ralph Bolton served on the camp committee, taught physiology in the school, preached sermons of high quality, laced with humour, and gave lectures guaranteed to hold his listeners' attention. Keith Gillison took an equally prominent part, playing the fool, as he dressed up for camp concerts, writing songs and parodies, grinding soya-beans for milk for the children, assisting with the French examinations in the school. Rob Symons, rather younger than Bolton and Gillison, went to the Saturday evening dances with the others of the youthful set. Dr. 'David' Gell, with her Eton crop of white hair, and brown skinned face, was admired and respected. The devotion of all four was obvious, so campers trusted them, as they trusted Matron Wheal, Nurse 'Jaggers' and the other nurses of the clinic and hospital. The system of regular medical examinations, and injections to ward off the diseases of the East: typhoid and cholera, paid off. The case of the Japanese appendix proved a fortunate accident, since the medics had a bargaining counter which secured medicines allowing them to do an effective job.

Moreover, there was a high ratio of doctors to patients: four doctors and a dentist served some six hundred and twenty individuals (the figure fluctuated somewhat during the 2½ years of internment). And this figure omits the nurses, essential to the smooth running of hospital and clinic. This high ratio bears comparison with the average ratio obtaining in England today: one G.P. to just over 1840 patients. This ratio is almost identical with the figure - 1:1800 - in the practice of Shropshire, where I now live. [24]

Next, our monotonous diet was supplemented by garden produce which we grew ourselves. The considerable tomato crop provided vitamins A, B and C. Gardeners distributed their vegetables among those who did not garden, for whatever reason. Distribution was sometimes in the form of gifts; sometimes vegetables and fruit were exchanged as a deal between campers: good old-fashioned barter. [25]

During a camp meeting, someone asked Dr. Bolton whether we had an adequate diet. His reply was *not* popular: he stated that the diet was boring and unpalatable, but it was sufficient to sustain life. Moreover, Yangchow had no cases of deficiency diseases, like scurvy or beri-beri, although many people were underweight. Ralph's speech apparently

> "generated some heat – full marks to Ralph for courage and honesty" [26]

The parcels we received from Shanghai had a two-fold benefit; the food itself, and the psychological benefit of expectation. Waiting for parcels to arrive was often protracted, but it created hope, and this lifted the spirits of all.

And last, most campers had a sensible attitude to their own health. Most people took some form of exercise even if this was only walking the half mile round the camp's perimeter. Married couples walked it, to talk over problems in relative privacy; young couples in love, or on the way to it, strolled round in dreamy mood, counting themselves lucky if there was a moon. The two Catholic priests walked it, to say their breviary. My father, or George Henderson, and Father Thornton walked it, their heads bent deep in theological debate. We children ran round it, on our treasure hunts, searching for arrows and clues. The camp's sporting activities – whether softball, cricket or anything else – even a tug-of-war – were equally good exercise, even though it was well-nigh impossible to have a shower afterwards. Mr. Quincey instituted early morning P.T. exercises, for boys.

"Campers realised it was up to themselves to safeguard against sickness, and the best safeguard was to keep fit." [27]

All the well-organised activities of camp helped maintain our health. Skinny we may have been in August 1945, but we were alive. Only young Geoff Manley's death seems attributable to internment; possibly the camp experience broke his spirit. [28]

Many people were desperately hungry, until our release by the American and British teams in September 1945.

Afterwards most people soon returned to normal, though a few were left with long-term problems, probably traceable to internment. For instance, Colin Henderson, aged 12 in 1945, had been infected with hepatitis; he carried the virus all his life. After leaving camp, in due course Colin became a pilot in the RAF. He was away from home when, some years later, his wife Brenda became seriously ill with hepatitis, a sexually transmitted illness. Brenda relates that a close friend who belonged to an evangelical group attached to the Hendersons' church came to visit her in hospital. The friend told Brenda the group had been praying for her, and would continue to do so. Some five days later, Brenda's blood test was clear of infection. Inevitably there was a cloud over the relationship between Colin and Brenda; she felt guilty, but for no good reason. Not long before Colin died, the consultant attending him asked his wife whether she had ever suffered from hepatitis. Brenda then related this story. The consultant's judgment was that Colin had carried the virus all his life, since infection picked up in Yangchow. Husband and wife were then reconciled; the shadow over their relationship vanished. [29]

Peter, my own brother, was so ill with pleurisy in the spring of 1946 that he had the following summer term off school. His lungs were so affected that he was deemed unfit for national service, at age 18, despite having played rugby and having made the first team at Eltham College, the public school originally founded for the sons of missionaries.

And my mother too was seriously ill, at much the same time, for some eight weeks. This too was probably attributable to the privations of Yangchow. We have seen Mrs. Beynon's recurrent health problems. Similarly Mr. Gray who entered camp with a heart condition, was in the camp hospital in April, and also in October 1943. At one time Gray was asked if he wished to return to Shanghai, on account of his illness, but he refused. My father visited him after the end of the war in a Shanghai hospital. His weak heart cannot have improved under Yangchow conditions. [30]

As for the state of others' health in the long term, I do not know: no-one followed up the medical history of Yangchow internees. Tracing the long-term effects of internment on former internees might well have been a fascinating study but in 1946 the world was intent on reconstruction. Determining what percentage of us suffered poor health as a direct result of internment is now impossible.

1. Gillison, *The Cross and Dragon*, p.163
2. Gillison, K., p.163
3. Willis, *I was among the Captives*, p.114
4. Gillison, K., p.163
5. Begley, N., op. cit., p.123
6. Beryl Piper, 10 March 1945
7. Begley, N., op. cit., p.129
8. Gilbert Manley, recollections, October 2002
9. HFW, entries for 31 August, 1 and 6 September 1943
10. Gillison, K., p. 162, and HFW 26 October 1943
11. Beryl Piper, diary 3 and 4 April 1945
12. Beryl Piper, 5 February 1945
13. Colin Palmer, recollections, July 2002
14. Keith Martin, recollections, and Colin Palmer, recollections, July 2002. The story is confirmed in N. Begley, op. cit., p.98 and p.126
15. HFW, 9 April 1943
16. HFW, 26 July 1943
17. WO 325/122 in P.R.O.
18. Imperial War Museum, letter dated December 1945.
19. HFW, 7 May 1945
20. Neil Begley, *An Australian's childhood in China*, pp.125-6
21. Walford Gillison, recollections, October 2002
22. HFW, 22 October 1945
23. Walford Gillison, recollections, October 2002
24. The figure of 1 G.P. to 1840 patients came from the British Medical Association, via Walford Gillison. I obtained the Shropshire figure from my own practice, October 2002.
25. Gillison, K. and HFH diary, passion
26. Colin Palmer, recollections, December 2002
27. Kenneth Gibson, recollections,
28. See Begley, op. cit., p.142, as well as entries for 3 September 1945, regarding Geoff's death, in diaries of Beryl Piper and HFW
29. Brenda Henderson, recollections, October 2002
30. HFW, entries for 15 April and 19 October 1943. Also for 20 October 1945

SCHOOLING

> "And then the whining schoolboy, with his satchel
> And shining morning face, creeping like snail
> Unwillingly to school"
> As You Like It
Act II, sc. VII

We are fortunate in having considerable documentation about Yangchow C schools, especially where students in the 15 – 18 age group are concerned. Both Zena Goodman and Beryl Piper were in this group, and kept journals, and the relevant section in Keith Martin's memoir also provides information from the student angle. Chris Willis' book includes experience of his teaching Science and Maths. My father's own diary also gives a teacher's viewpoint; though he was not a trained teacher, he was a 'natural', and starts to write of 'my students' in the possessive fashion adopted by all teachers who love their profession. Apart from these sources, many people from younger age groups have touched on their experience of the camp's schools. There are certificates, exam papers, a few school reports, and other documents. It is a rich quarry.

Many of the camp's parents were impatient to see the establishment of schools for their children, in the unpromising circumstances of internment.

"Wish a school would begin …" My father's comment will have been echoed by most other parents of lively children, whose energies needed direction into constructive channels. [1] A few days later he was constructing a folding-stool for Peter, my brother, since the rule was that children had to take their own seats. There is no record of a stool for me, but I too went with big brother. "Not easy – made out of bits and pieces" commented my father. [2] We young ones, I was 5, Peter just 7, started our camp schooling in the baggage-room; other classes were held in the dining-room, or outside, in good weather. The boys' classes were, for a time, in the church building.

Ninety-eight children, aged under 16, were present in camp, needing education. [3] Clearly this was a priority for the authorities to arrange. Where the school was to be, proved something of a problem. Most classes were held at the tables in the big Assembly hall, which served as the camp dining-room. Some of the senior boys worked at their studies in part of the church building and, later, in a small room of a mud-floored gatehouse. So most teachers had to work hard, against competition from other activities, to secure their classes' attention. Chris Willis learnt that the really hard thing about teaching was to make oneself heard:

> "The camp office and stenographers were just behind the boys: the Latin class within three feet of the back of the Fourth form … supposed to be learning Maths … The Fifth was having an interesting story read aloud for their English lesson; just at the back … were the billets, little cubicles divided off by curtains or straw mats, where the ladies would often be holding an exciting conversation."

Once again, cramped conditions challenged the skill of the camp's teachers. [4]

Yet another serious problem was lack of equipment, especially of paper. Many former internees remember doing sums, writing notes, practising their grammar, on old labels from jam-jars. Some boys raided the garbage for tin-can labels, so as to do their homework.

> "Most families had brought toilet paper, so the children brought and used that at school and then took it home … for the use it had been designed for." [5]

Younger children like me, aged 6 or 7, could practise their letters on old-fashioned slates. How heavy they were, in their worn wooden frames, and how easy it was to annoy one's teacher, by squeaking one's slate pencil! Major difficulties were the lack of dictionaries for language teaching, and lack of basic laboratory equipment. Nonetheless most teachers, professional or co-opted, took such difficulties as challenges to be overcome, and so the standard of teaching was high.

Fortune, or perhaps the B.R.A. in Shanghai, was kind to us in Yangchow C. Two fine headteachers, Rev. P. C. Matthews and Miss Joan Penfold, were responsible for the boys and girls. P.C.M. had to persuade many of the camp's graduates to act as teachers in the Boys' school, and sometimes in the Girls' school, as well. Chris Willis, with his B.Sc. from McGill, was cajoled into teaching science. When he protested his complete lack of experience, Willis was told there was no-one else:

> "And so the work fell on my shoulders." [6]

My father, with his Edinburgh arts degree, was in similar case. He had taught history to the senior girls, before Christmas 1943. Then P. C. Matthews co-opted him to the senior boys, for English and History, following a row over the standard of these subjects. Many parents complained about the teaching of Bill Kemp, and H. W. Ray:

> "Educ. Com. ('cos of letter of protest … from parents re Kemp and Ray). Bolton and I interviewed Kemp. Thornton and Bolton saw Ray. So now I must teach Eng. Lit. and Hist. to senior boys." [7]

As for P. C. Matthews, formerly in charge of the Cathedral Boys' school in Shanghai, he was intimidating. Lads like Walford Gillison and the two Bolton boys were terrified of him. Even Keith Martin, starting Latin from scratch at the Cathedral school, was scared of the Head, with his first-class classics degree. The boys ran off to the cloakroom before each Latin class, to spruce themselves up, and sleek down their hair. As

Yangchow Years

Keith matured into the VIth form at Yangchow, he became more appreciative of P.C.M., so much so that when Keith married, he invited his former Headmaster to perform the ceremony. But Neil Begley voiced the opinion of the younger lads, when he wrote:

> "We lived in more fear of him (P. C. Matthews) than we did of the Japs. He used his cane with abandon ... although he petrified us, we all agreed he was absolutely fair."

But not everyone agrees. Albert Nissim recalls:

> "He was very anti-Jewish and took it out on many of us in a nasty and physical manner." [8]

In the Girls' school, Miss Penfold, with her bachelor's degree from London University, was head. She had been a senior teacher in the Shanghai Cathedral Girls' school, where her sister was head, before being interned in Lunghua. "Penny", as our Yangchow girls termed her, recognised how difficult it was to study in the bitter cold of January. She would send the girls outside to run around, and get their circulation going again. Penny herself taught wearing a fur coat, and pixie hood. [9]

Other teachers were fully trained professionals, some with considerable experience. Molly Bolton, Ralph's sister, was an expert in French. Betty James, a brilliant History teacher in the eyes of Walford Gillison, one of her younger pupils, had an English Literature degree from London. Kath Gillison, wife to Keith, the camp surgeon, taught Latin and Maths to the older girls. Her previous teaching experience was in Plymouth, Co. Devon. Teaching Latin without a dictionary must have been taxing. Fortunately a Latin dictionary eventually arrived, thanks to the Red Cross. This highlights the textbook problem. Cathedral School boys were told, before internment, to take some text books, to share with fellow-students. Keith Martin took Kennedy's Latin Primer, a volume on Latin composition, and some mathematical tables. [10]

By contrast with P. C. Matthews, Joan Penfold inspired respect, and some affection from the girls. Brenda Smith, about 12 years old in camp, thought her very fair. Miss Penfold was younger than P.C.M., only 34, compared to his 51, when the war ended. There will have been only sixteen years' age difference between Miss Penfold, and the eldest girls, and this will have eased their relationship. A further contrast in ages was between Mona Nissim and I, youngest in the school, and terrifying Miss Wagstaff, who was fifty years our senior. Ethel Wagstaff, head of kindergarten, was dark. Everything about her was black, or nearly so, from her black-rimmed spectacles, and dark hair, to her piercing eyes. Under the glare from those spectacles, we had to sit up very straight on the hard benches, and fold our arms, before she would release us at the end of school, to scamper homewards.

"Intimidating" is the adjective which best describes Ethel Wagstaff. Dark-haired and dark-browed, she was an exacting teacher, whose high standards it was difficult to satisfy. Her methods were, by modern standards, old-fashioned; chalk and talk: exposition by the teacher, followed by children's practice of the rule, whether in English grammar, or in mathematics. We had spelling bees, attempted the mysteries of parsing, and long division, and learnt our Shakespeare from Lamb's Tales. Some poetry I have for life: "Full fathom five thy father lies", "Come unto these yellow sands", among the poems engraved on my memory, associated inextricably with the hard benches of Yangchow dining-hall.

I learnt French, from age 6. "Madame Souris a une maison" we learnt to chant in Form 1C. Someone had brought a child's reading-book, complete with pictures. Mme. Souris was evidently a bourgeoise; we learnt much about her possessions. Learning French was taken for granted, just as was my brother Peter's starting Latin at age 8.

Older boys, David Bolton and Peter Gibson, were shining lights in the classroom:

> "Peter Gibson and I competed for top place in each subject – he won most times."

Then both were promoted to the boys' class, where their elder brothers, Tom Bolton and Kenny Gibson were. Boys sat in class in order of achievement. Peter soon overtook Kenny, but Tom, older than David, by some two years, kept young brother in his place. [11]

Latin seems to have been of great significance to these boys. P. C. Matthews was very strict in his treatment of Latin unseens. Any boy who made a mistake had to revise the entire exercise, on paper, peeled from old tin cans. Pronunciation of Latin was controversial. Sometimes Father Thornton would stand in and take a class for P.C. His Latin pronunciation was old-fashioned church style. David Bolton was insatiably curious; he was fired by an ambition to learn Greek as well as Latin. He endeavoured to persuade Mr. Willis to instruct him in Greek, starting with the Gospel of Mark. The Willis family, including Helen, sister to Chris, had brought some Greek Lexicons into camp, along with other texts. She had obviously been told to expect a good deal of leisure time, which never materialised. [12]

The English teaching for these young lads was memorable:

> "We were told … to read a Scott or Dickens novel every week! And astonishingly I kept it up for some time … I remember reading "The Hobbit" and dismissing it as ridiculous." [13]

His class had to learn an *Ode to a Skylark*, *Gray's Elegy*, some of Milton's sonnets and Coleridge's *Ancient Mariner*, by heart, from *Palgrave's Golden Treasury*. And he still knows them, and can recite these poems at length. A gift for life. Father Thornton was:
> "an inspiring teacher of English. I can still hear him reading *Treasure Island* to an enthralled group of 10 and 11 year olds."

This was the opinion of Peter Gibson, then a bright youngster and friendly rival to David Bolton. Peter's curiosity was aroused by the North China Daily News, which was posted on the notice board by the back gate, near his classroom. He read the news, with its pro-Japanese slant, and then looked up all the places which were mentioned, in an atlas. In this way he located the battlegrounds in Russia, or North Africa, and the sea-battles in the Pacific. At the same time, he enlarged his geographical knowledge. [14]

His knowledge will have been far sounder than my own. Geography was total confusion to me; which city, Nanking or Peking was the capital of China? Maps always seemed to have the land-locked Caspian Sea as their main feature. It was sufficiently remote from Yangchow, or Shanghai, and even more remote from England, where my grandparents lived. The rivalry between Peter Gibson and David Bolton must have dissipated for, years later, they played squash together at Oxford. [15]

With no laboratory, teaching science to these 10 – 12 year olds was difficult. According to David Bolton:

> "Mr. Willis took us for what he called science, but was the workings of the piston pump, the force pump and the hydraulic ram. The Science master at my English school was nonplussed about this."

Nonetheless David learned enough "science" to become a doctor in time. So too did his elder brother, Tom and Walford Gillison, as well. Phyllis Box, in Lunghua camp, also became a doctor. She found her internment camp experience beneficial:

> "Science – into the grounds surrounding the classrooms, catch your frog, chloroform it and dissect, making accurate drawings."

Phyllis was one of Lunghua's goatherds; their goats' milk fed the camp's babies. [16]

Despite internment, and the absence of normal school facilities, the camp authorities made every effort to give us children a sound education. This was particularly important for young people in their teens, soon to embark on their careers. In these challenging circumstances both Miss Penfold and P. C. Matthews knew that boys and girls aged 16 to 18 would need the equivalent of a School Leaving Certificate, if they were to pursue careers in the post-war world. This was the thinking behind their co-option of people who might lack experience as teachers, but who had knowledge or skills to impart. The diaries of Zena Goodman and Beryl Piper show how hard these girls studied. Of course they played hard too, and of that more elsewhere. Time and again we find Beryl, Zena, Vera Litter and Joan Beynon studying out "at the back", that is, behind their accommodation block. One afternoon they would be studying French, taught by Miss Molly Bolton, or Miss Morton-Smith. Sometimes there would be history tutorials with my father. Fay Westwood, friend to Carol Parry, was in a younger class, but she too loved history:

> "He [my father'] was witty, with a merry twinkle in his penetrating blue (sic) eyes. Indeed history soon became my favourite subject. In reviewing the ancient lore of the Vikings, the invasions of Britain by the Picts and Scots, and the foundations of Magna Carta, we became good friends."

Since both their surnames began with W, Fay soon started to stand near him in the dinner queue:

> "Here we could further develop a thought begun in the class discussions … despite what he called my "atrocious spelling" he thought highly enough of my history essays to take a personal interest in me." [17]

Our classes were small; School Certificate groups averaged 13 students in the Boys' School; tutorial groups, with two or three students, often met outside in good weather. In the kindergarten I was one of eight pupils. Individual help was often available: Beryl Piper was coached in Maths by Mr. Willis. He was good enough to teach my brother Peter sketching and the art of perspective, when Peter was recovering from an attack of broncho-pneumonia. [18]

Details of the School Certificate exam had to be introduced to the co-opted teachers. P. C. Matthews explained them to my father. Exams were taken seriously: papers were jointly prepared, and jointly marked. Miss Willis and my father composed the English papers together, language and literature, as he did with Betty James, for history.

Betty, young and attractive, with a London B.A., was a brilliant teacher, whose history lessons figure large in Walford Gillison's memory. Dad even taught some geography, co-operating with Miss Jeffaris, who had a Liverpool M.Sc. degree. [19]

Exams were the usual ordeal for the students. But the results - School Certificate in the summer 1944 – were a triumph. Eleven candidates passed, five with marks sufficiently high to secure university entrance: Joan Beynon, Ted Evans, Keith Martin, Colin Palmer and Ken Shirazee. Their question papers were sent to Cambridge after the war, and the results validated by the university authorities. The students were fortunate in the commitment of their teachers.

> "The missionaries … provided … the best scholastic and moral education they could give." [20]

There was no professional mathematician, though a leading Shanghai accountant, Ernie Hardman, taught higher maths beyond School Certificate standard.

> "He dazzled his students by teaching them shortcuts, such as multiplying five or more digits, by five or more digits on a single line." [21]

The Beryl Piper episode is especially fascinating. Initially it seemed she had failed the entire exam, because of failing her French paper. Beryl warned herself not to panic, but nerves overtook her, when Miss Penfold instructed the girls to take writing materials to the exam room. Beryl had fever during the French exam. Kind Mr. Willis, the invigilator, brought her coffee and fanned her throughout the exam. Despite this, Beryl and her parents were devastated by her failure. A fresh reading of the Syllabus allowed her to pass.

> "Able to pass Beryl Piper: great rejoicing." So wrote my father. "Mr. Wickings came and explained the whole thing." So wrote Beryl. [22]

The tone of Beryl's diary alters from despair to elation, as the candidates prepared for Speech Day. Dressed in white, the girls, Joan Beynon, Valerie Judah, Vera Litter and Beryl herself, collected their certificates first. Beryl, lacking a white skirt, had to borrow one. The boys followed.

This festive occasion concluded with plays. The last was the trial scene from *The Merchant of Venice*, produced out of doors in the summer sunshine. Valerie Judah starred as Portia, graceful in my father's black gown. I, an impressionable six-year old, heard the 'Quality of mercy' speech for the first time. Bassanio (Teddy Evans) and Antonio (Colin Palmer) swaggered in their bright silk costumes. The duke's solitary figure, Keith Martin, majestic in purple, dominated the trial from his high throne. A memorable scene.

> "Exceedingly good. Proud of my scholars", commented my father. [23]

Never lavish with praise, my father considered further dramatic events. Later in August he found another play: Bernard Shaw's *Androcles and the Lion*, his adopted script ran to fifteen foolscap pages of typing. Not surprisingly, he commented:

"Now my left shoulder gives trouble." [24]

The Merchant of Venice was not the first Shakespeare play performed by the school. The year before, 1943, the boys' school produced scenes from *Twelfth Night* on Speech Day. It is easy to understand why this play was chosen; only two parts were female roles: the Lady Olivia, and the soubrette Maria. So only Colin Palmer (Olivia) and Geoff Manley (Maria, the maid) had to cross-dress, as in Shakespeare's own day. The commandant, Hashizumi, presented certificates to those winning form prizes. Many of these certificates have survived as the treasured possessions of those who won them. Four senior boys also received handsome carved prefects' badges: Kenny Shirazee, Reg Phillips, Teddy Evans and Keith Martin, Teddy's close friend. In 1945 Chris Day and Gordon Savage became prefects, too.

Yangchow students valued their education. Keith Martin relates how he was summoned by the Japanese commandant, who had heard from Keith's mother, that she wanted Keith and his sister June, to join her in Stanley camp, Hong Kong. Mrs. Jewell, Keith's aunt, accompanied him to the interview, but was forbidden to speak. Keith considered this offer with care. He had learnt that conditions in Stanley were worse than those in Yangchow. Moreover, School Certificate exams were to be held the following summer. This would be a good qualification both for him, and later, for June, who was benefiting from camp education. Finally, he had heard, before internment, that American submarines were sinking Japanese vessels along the coast of China; if he accepted the commandant's offer of places on such a vessel, he and June would be in danger. For all these reasons, Keith decided that he and June would stay at Yangchow; a tough decision for a young man of 15 to take.

Yangchow Years

The commandant remarked in Japanese:

"You have made a wise decision."

Mrs. Martin will have been the person to suffer most, when the ship docked in Hong Kong, without June and Keith, her children. [25]

Occasional tensions marred the industry of the Boys' and Girls' schools. George Henderson had orchestrated the parental protest over the standard of English teaching by Messrs. Ray and Kemp. Soon after, Mr. Willis' strict adherence to the wording of the Bible made for difficulty in his Science classes. He took the Creation story in Genesis absolutely literally, and made repeated references to it in the boys' science lessons. A circular was despatched to all teachers:

"<u>Only those staff teaching English literature should refer to the Bible in their lessons.</u>"

The edict provoked Willis' resignation, and created a problem for the Headmaster, since no-one else was qualified to undertake the Science teaching. A compromise was effected. The education committee "graciously decided that I could continue where necessary to refer to the Bible". The irony of the situation was that Willis did not scruple to impose the writing of lines on naughty boys, and used to make them copy lines from Scripture, since corporal punishment was banned. After this token resignation Willis continued to teach until our release. [26]

The headteachers must have found it difficult to administer their schools. They had to deal with teachers who were individuals of strong convictions, and also instruct them in the complexities of School Certificate exams. Beautifully lettered certificates issued by the school are preserved by some of its former students, Keith Martin among them. The actual wording of the certificates emanated from the school authorities; my father passed on the wording to George Manley, whose artistic talent was considerable. Reports were issued for younger children too. I still have some termly reports, typed on thin fine paper. They give term and exam marks, and comment adversely on my handwriting, then the worst aspect of my school work, since Peter and I were both bright children, at or near the top of our respective classes.

Vocational classes for school-leavers marked the last academic year. Shorthand was taught by Mrs. Corneck, previously head of her own secretarial college in Shanghai. Zena Goodman and Beryl Piper attended as did some of the young men: Ken Shirazee and Keith Martin among them. Ernie Hardman and Cecil Longhurst gave accountancy classes; Keith Martin retains his certificate of proficiency in double-entry bookkeeping; Longhurst and Hardman signed it, and Skipper Grant counter-signed. Hardman, so respected as an accountant, had to battle against cataract in both eyes. Chris Willis met him after our release, in Shanghai. Hardman was:

> "as proud as could be to tell of the remarkable successes of nearly all our students ... " [27]

Other vocational classes were those on anatomy and physiology taught by Drs. Gillison and Bolton. They were intended for those embarking on medical careers.

The Vth and VIth forms continued their academic studies, with some students attending the vocational classes described above. A trio of girls: June Martin, Rosalie Duckitt and Jean Dickson had tutorials with my father. He started to feel the pressure of teaching commitments, preparation for them, and for his six Bible classes, plus essay-marking. Mondays were exceptionally busy – the day of my mother's stint in the camp kitchen - so the care of Peter and me, after school was over, fell to him.

The winter of January 1945 was especially cold; roll call, normally outside, was abolished for ten days. Then the electricity supply failed; candle-light alone was available for students' homework, and teachers' preparation.

Yangchow Years

Peter and I sat on our father's knee, as he read our bedtime story, by candle light. All homework stopped, for the duration.

Though the lights did not work properly till May, term resumed in April. Intense competition between Joan Beynon and Keith Martin for the top place meant they tied for it at half-term. The final VIth form result showed Joan as first, with Keith a few marks behind. My father commented:

> "Yet all the boys have done hard labour (well-digging etc.) while she [Joan] had leisure to swot in afternoons." [28]

Lively, intelligent Joan had worked hard, alongside Zena Goodman and Vera Litter, her close friends. The camp nicknamed them the Vamps, while my father termed them the Three Graces. As form-master to the VIth, he and my mother entertained all of them to tea, in their classroom.

The education committee had provided a Qualifying exam for Vth formers, lest the camp did not exist in November, as a venue for School Certificate. The results were mixed; my father told Gordon Savage's parents he had passed, but recoiled at the prospect of meeting disappointed parents of those who had failed:

> "Feel that I should like some other job than teaching." [29]

One tribute to the quality of teaching given us was the link established between teachers and taught. In 1961, Rev. P. C. Matthews performed the marriage ceremony of Keith Martin to Sarah, Keith's bride. My father was invited to marry Marjorie Train to Lawrence Lee in 1952. He was also asked to preach at Ann Silver's wedding; both brides had belonged to his Bible classes in Yangchow.

Many of us, later on, made it through the system, reaching the professions, medical school, university and college. To cite but a few: Peter Gibson became an eminent judge, Colin Palmer an ophthalmologist, while both

Bolton sons and Walford Gillison followed their fathers into medical careers. Keith Martin held a highly responsible position in Shell. Rosalie Duckitt became a solicitor, after Girton, Cambridge. Gilbert Manley entered academia specialising in biological anthropology, while his brother Owen eventually ended up as head of his department at Rolls-Royce in Coventry. Peter Jewell and Colin Henderson both became RAF pilots; latterly Colin worked with drug-addicts as a matter of social concern. Peter read history at Emanuel College, Cambridge, while I, too, read history at Lady Margaret Hall, Oxford.

School, makeshift though it was, was one of the best aspects of Yangchow life. Methods like English dictation, and much learning by heart, are now thought old-fashioned. But we children were not deprived of our English heritage, despite being immured by the Japanese. We learnt to co-operate, to perform in concerts and plays, to enjoy disciplined activities. School was fun, to quote David Bolton, despite the cold, our chilblains, summer humidity, the lack of texts and materials. My father sometimes confided to his diary, his fear that his children were missing proper schooling. There was no need; we were sufficiently grounded when we reached home. The concern of parents for their youngsters' education was a positive emotion. The camp simply had to invest effort and commitment into the welfare of its children. We were, after all, the future.

1. HFW, 1 April 1943
2. HFW, 5 April 1943
3. Camp list, 8 March, 1944
4. Willis, p.103
5. Gillison, *The Cross and the Dragon*, p.161
6. Willis, p.102
7. HFW, 1 January 1944
8. Walford Gillison and Keith Martin, recollections, June 2002. Neil Begley, pp.109 and 111. Albert Nissim, recollections, December 2002.
9. Carol Parry, recollections, August 2002
10. Gillison, p.161; Walford Gillison, recollections, June 2002; and Keith Martin, recollections, October 2002.
11. David Bolton, recollections, June 2002
12. Willis, p.108
13. David Bolton, recollections, June 2002
14. Peter Gibson, recollections, September 2002
15. David Bolton recollections, June 2002, and Peter Gibson, recollections, September 2002
16. David Bolton, recollections and Phyllis Box, recollections, both June 2002
17. Angus, *White Pagoda*, p.138
18. PRW, recollections, June 2002
19. HFW, 7 July and 4 August 1944 and Walford Gillison, recollections, June 2002
20. Albert Nissim, recollections, December 2002
21. Angus, *White Pagoda*, p.126
22. HFW and Beryl Piper, entries for 15 August 1944
23. HFW, 15 August 1944
24. HFW, 28 August 1944
25. Keith Martin, unpublished memoir, p.14
26. Willis, p.107 and HFW, 7 February 1944
27. Willis, p.122
28. HFW, 30 June 1945
29. HFW, 11 July 1945

RELIGION

"That they may all be one ..."   St. John, c.17, v.1
"See how these Christians love one another ... "

During the confused month of February 1943, the British Residents' Association of Shanghai had arranged the provision of religious leadership for the various camps. Also there were to be leaders for all faiths: Catholics, Protestants in great variety and Jews. Only the White Russians of the Orthodox Church had no leader of their own. So we in Yangchow had two Catholic priests, a single ordained Anglican, and three Free Churchmen to minister to their respective communities.

From the outset, the Catholics had daily Mass, celebrated in the camp dining hall. The Protestants united for Sunday services. The only Church of England clergyman was Rev. P. C. Matthews, an important figure in the camp, since he was also head of the boys' school. The three Free Churchmen were all missionaries: Major Begley of the Salvation Army, Rev. George Henderson, a Scottish Presbyterian, and my own father, Rev. Harold Wickings, from the London Missionary Society. Besides these four ordained men, there were other missionaries, of both sexes. And there was Chris Willis – the evangelical – whose book gives its own distinctive view of Yangchow C. [1]

The Catholic Community

Father O'Collins and Father Thornton, the two Catholic priests, were a strong contrast to one another. Father Michael O'Collins, from Australia, well into middle age, arrived a month after most other internees, in April 1943. Father James Thornton, a young Jesuit, joined him two months later. He was to have a strong influence on the young people of the camp. The Catholic community was potentially larger than the 30 or so people who regularly attended Mass. [2]

The influence of tall, dark, gaunt Father Jim, as he was soon to be called, radiated far beyond the immediate Catholic community. Father Jim was a sportsman, keen on softball, which soon became a favourite sport of the camp's teenagers. The young priest was part way through his Jesuit training. Father O'Collins had a goatee beard; his shock of white hair contrasted with Father Jim's dark head, as they walked round the boundary, saying their daily Office.

Mass was said and the most faithful attended daily. Occasionally there was Benediction too, with the Angelus. Initially it was difficult to avoid tension between Catholics and Protestants over the timing of services in the dining hall, but this was soon ironed out.

The Church of England

In one sense the Anglicans were unfortunate, as PCM was its only ordained priest. He conducted matins, and preached a sermon every other Sunday, as the pattern of services alternated with other Protestant services. At first this will have been taxing for PCM, as he became known. The strain on him was considerable; he could not afford to be ill on Sunday, whereas the Free Churchmen could always substitute for one another. PCM was a bachelor, around 50 years old. He had considerable influence, as he combined the roles of headmaster, and Anglican priest. Initially, he feared that Anglican traditions might be swamped. This fear was unnecessary as the Church of England's presence was sufficiently strong for the Bishop of Shantung, Rt. Rev. John Wellington, to confirm fourteen candidates in July 1943. Bishop Wellington was interned in Yangchow B, before its inmates were transferred to Shanghai. One of the candidates, Keith Martin, retains his confirmation certificate to this day. [3]

The 1662 Prayer Book service of Holy Communion was celebrated on Sundays, with a dozen or fifteen regular communicants. Many more attended the mid-morning service – probably fifty or sixty on average. But this was a combined service of most Protestant traditions. Its congregation grew steadily, as time went on. Fewer people attended the evening service, where Evensong in the Anglican fashion alternated with a Free Church service. [4]

The Free Churches

My father was the official Free Church chaplain, selected by the B.R.A. But he was fortunate in having George Henderson, from the Scottish Presbyterian tradition, as a colleague. George was a key figure in camp. He learnt to work with people from "all walks of life, and various shades of religious belief at all sorts of menial tasks". He even led matins in approved Anglican form, when PCM was ill. Writing in August 1945 and looking back, George stated:

> "A goodly number of young folks joined both Anglican and Free Church communions … while many previous non-churchgoers have become regular attenders."

Major Begley and Edith, his wife, both Australians, represented the Salvation Army. Major Begley preached regularly. The Free Church respect for exposition of the Bible was particularly well upheld: both my father's sermons, and the lively preaching of Dr. Ralph Bolton, of the Methodist Missionary Society, were commended by their hearers. If we are to believe my father's diary, he did endeavour to keep his sermons short, and was very critical of others who preached too long, especially in cold weather.

The Evangelicals

Some evangelicals with a fundamentalist outlook attended these Protestant services regularly. Among them was the Parry family; F. E.

Parry was Camp Secretary for the latter part of our internment. The family was friendly with Chris Willis, the Canadian whose Gospel chorus services drew some of the camp's children. These sessions were separate from the more conventional Sunday School. Nor did any of the three Willis family attend the Bible classes taught by my father, or those of Ralph Bolton. Mr. Willis was a skilled artist, who had brought paints and sketching materials with him. His custom was to present his acquaintance with colourful scrolls, blazoned with Gospel texts. My parents received one for Easter 1943. But in worship, Chris Willis, his wife and sister kept apart from the other Protestants, who were striving to achieve a measure of church unity.

Relationships and Tensions

Father Thornton managed to be on good terms with most other Christians. Though different in theological outlook, Chris Willis counted Father James as one of his best friends, and this despite Catholic teaching on the Virgin Mary, which Willis thought idolatry. Willis and Thornton walked and talked together, just as George Henderson did with Fr. Thornton. Henderson valued the practical help which he gave:

> "You could see a Catholic priest in overalls and clerical collar helping to stoke the kitchen fires or, with cassock girt up round his waist, grinding soya beans with a stone hand-mill." [5]

George commanded respect from his fellow internees, so much so that he was trusted to be in charge of the camp's food store. This was a tribute to his integrity as well as a responsibility, for the position meant he had to stop petty pilfering. Indeed, George contributed to camp life in many ways: he had cleaned loos, stoked fires and carried coal, before the kitchen job. Here he supervised more than 90 people in the kitchen teams, and oversaw the supply and serving of food to the entire camp. Somehow, too, he found time to be the camp barber, both for men and women. As he later wrote:

> "Many a time ... I have been devoutly thankful for my early upbringing in the far North of Scotland where a lad was expected to tackle [any task] without demur." [5]

As for my father, his regard for Father Thornton grew, as the prejudice he had inherited against Catholicism gradually melted. Obviously they retained their basic Catholic and Protestant beliefs, but each began to understand the other's tradition. Dad was not convinced by the Catholic attitude to Scripture. Probably both Fr. O'Collins and Fr. Thornton found the Protestant stress on the Bible's centrality equally puzzling. After 1945, and our liberation, Fr. Thornton and my father never met again, though they did correspond. A letter, in 1990, from California, where Fr. Thornton ministered to a Chinese community, survives. He signs himself "Your brother in Christ". I like to think their friendship, begun in time, continues in eternity. [6]

Some impressionable young people abandoned their own original faith. One of these was convent-educated Fay Westwood, aged sixteen, who had been brought up as a Catholic. Her admirer, Gordon Savage, was a Protestant influence on her. So, too, was my father, whose exposition of Scripture impressed all who attended his Bible classes. Fay used her proximity to my father in the dinner queue – since both their surnames began with 'W' – to discuss topics which arose in history class. [7]

Initially there was some tension between Protestants and Catholics. Mrs. Rees, a Catholic, whose only child, Sonny, had died in camp, discussed the need to reduce friction between the two groups with my father. The uneasy relationship cannot have been helped by Chris Willis' circulation of anti-Catholic pamphlets:

> "A talk with O'Collins and Thornton re anti-RC tracts issued by G. C. Willis – the man a fanatic." [8]

Chris Willis and my father were chalk and cheese. Both were direct individuals forthright in their speech and accustomed to declaring the truth as they saw it. Their views were found to clash, as my father's scholarly attitude to the Bible conflicted with Willis' literal interpretation of it. One instance will suffice: one of the boys asked Willis to explain St. Matthew's account of Palm Sunday, when Jesus rode into Jerusalem on "an ass and the foal of an ass". This was, of course, a trick question. Were there, asked the lad, two beasts? Imagine the boy's delight when, after some thought, Willis replied that he ass must have been pregnant.

Willis antagonised others, too, by placing his finely illuminated texts in the camp dining room. He claimed to have had the permission of 'Skipper' Grant, but the camp committee forbade his posting more texts without their specific permission. The committee feared the texts' evangelical nature could antagonise those who did not share Willis' evangelical views. Willis suffered persecution mania, but continued to give texts as presents to friends, so the texts were hung in some private rooms. [9]

The clash between Willis' fundamentalist outlook, and my father's, relying on Biblical scholarship, was profound. It recurred on the explosive topic of Hell, sparked off by a talk given by P. C. Matthews, during the Sunday evening discussions. A week later Willis, at his own request, expounded his own view of Eternal Punishment. My father held his tongue, believing it was useless to argue with Willis. [10]

Despite the difference in "theological" outlook, Mr. Willis was generous in spirit, and especially kind to my brother. Peter, aged 9, was recovering from broncho-pneumonia. He was languid and bored. Mr. Willis spared the time to teach Peter to draw, teaching him the rules of perspective. Willis' suspicion of the "modernist" father did not prevent his goodness to the young son. Peter recalls Willis' kindness to this day. [11]

Bible Classes

From their inception the Bible classes led by my father were popular. The first was a mixed group of men and women, studying the Acts of the Apostles. Soon there were separate classes for men and women, to fit in with the various tasks undertaken by all able-bodied internees. By November 1944, he was leading six classes each week; this involved a good deal of preparation time. Then the young ladies' class grew too large for genuine discussion; it was divided into a class for elder girls nicknamed the "Cats", and a younger group known as the "Kittens". [12]

Meantime others, like Ralph Bolton, held their own classes to study scripture. Ralph Bolton dealt with younger lads than those in my father's group of young men. Major Begley had a class too, from the Salvationist standpoint. As for Mr. Willis, he held Gospel chorus sessions for children on Sunday afternoons. Roman Catholic children were forbidden to attend these, by their priest. And my father, too, preferred Peter and me to look at Bible pictures with him, since he wanted to protect us from the "blood and fire" choruses sung there. [13]

Lay participation

From the beginning the laity played a big part in determining the camp's religious activities. Six laymen, all articulate, formed a significant group on the ministers' committee: Dr. Ralph Bolton; his fellow-medic Rob Symons; Joe Evans, the Welsh choirmaster; Owen Beynon, also Welsh the pharmacist; and Cecil Longhurst, the camp accountant. The only lady member was Ethel Wagstaff, the head of the kindergarten. All these people will have expressed decided views on matters of worship, and also of organisation. In the last few months of our Yangchow life Keith Martin, still in his late teens, was selected for membership of this committee. His friends teased him mercilessly for belonging to this august body. Laymen were encouraged to preach at Protestant Services – Mr. Longhurst did so more than once, and Ralph Bolton was a star. [14]

Women

Women were prominent in church activities: for instance, Betty James, young and intelligent, described "Hymns with a history", while Eileen

Bolton spoke on J. S. Bach's music, in a Sunday evening session. Edith Begley, of the Salvation Army, produced our nativity plays, besides acting as nurse, and mother. The London Missionary Society regarded married couples as twosomes and paid them a joint salary. At Siaokan, my mother had led a women's Bible class, and played the church organ. Single ladies like Hilda Shepherd were equally valued; at Yangchow she was a nursing sister, helping train new orderlies like Beryl Piper. Gwen Morris, friend and colleague of Betty James, taught Mandarin Chinese to such adults as wished to learn, despite the sciatica which kept her in hospital for long periods. An important reason for feminine participation was the preponderance of women over men at Yangchow: they outnumbered the men by some one hundred persons. [15]

Choir

Both my parents sang in the choir, my mother as an alto, my father among the basses. They were all carried along by the Celtic dynamism of J. J. Evans, the choirmaster, whose son, Teddy, was Keith Martin's friend from Cathedral School days. Vyvyan Dent played the organ, with George Kemp able to take over if Mr. Dent was ill. The choir rehearsed regularly, often in strange places – such as the boathouse or, in summer, outside. Occasionally some Catholics joined for a specific purpose, as happened at Christmas 1944 when everyone rehearsed carols together. My father was one of two basses in an octet, hidden from view, which produced Christmas music for the nativity scenes.

The Welsh carol – Poverty – was one of Joe Evans' favourites:

> "All poor men and humble, all lame men who stumble
> Come haste ye, nor feel ye afraid.
> For Jesus our treasure, with love past all measure
> In lowly poor stable was laid."

He taught it to the choir; it was peculiarly apposite to our camp situation, where all of us, from whatever background, shared many deprivations and anxieties about families and friends far away.

Russian Orthodox

"Christos vos kreisey! Christ is risen!"

The triumphant shout on Easter Day from the people, responding to their priest's greeting.

"Christ is risen!" proclaims the priest. "He is risen indeed" reply the people.

The Russian Orthodox community in Yangchow had no priest of its own, so they asked my father to give the greeting on this greatest of Church feasts. Yes, he agreed, but only if one of them would coach his pronunciation. For a short time, he formed part of the Orthodox tradition. The Russian ladies' choir sang an anthem at the united service, that first Easter. Later, a special cake – kulich – was shared, and a piece given to my parents. [16]

The Orthodox Christians were White Russians, from Shanghai. Most were wives of British servicemen or business people. Holding British passports, they were interned with the rest of us. Mrs. Olga Linkhorn is a good example; she was the widow of A. B. Linkhorn, one of six crew members killed when the Japanese sunk H.M.S. Peterel, at the time of Pearl Harbour. [17]

In 1944 it was Rev. P. C. Matthews' turn to proclaim the Easter greeting. He had placed two icons on the altar; his sermon referred to Archbishop Temple's visit to Moscow, possibly a sign of reduced Soviet hostility to religion, and to Europeans. [18]

The Jewish community

The flourishing community of Jews comprised some fifty adults, and nine children, rather more women – 33 than men – 17. Their surnames are obvious from the camp lists: Solomon, Moses, Levy and Nissim are instantly recognisable. Many were Sephardic Jews, including the two Nissim families. I was friendly with Rachel and Mona, the youngest Nissims; why could they not come out to play with the rest of us on Saturdays? What was Shabbat – whatever did it mean?

The Jews made a strong self-contained group. As the Chosen People they held themselves somewhat apart, with a separate kitchen, and separate kitchen utensils. The orthodox among them had double quantities of vegetables, as pork was the only meat available, and they could not eat it. The most orthodox took the counterpane from his bed, to launder it, when a Gentile brushed past, so rendering it unclean. [19]

But Jewish young people and children were friends with the rest of us. Where would the camp have been without Matty Nissim's bugle-call each morning?

> "Oh, it's good to get up in the morning.
> It's better to stay in bed …"

Eddie Weidman, Matty and the other Nissims played bridge, went to dances, and played softball along with everyone else. Albert Nissim shared the boys' passion for birds' nesting, while Rachel and Mona were fellow-Brownies with me.

Obviously the Jews worshipped apart, and instructed their children with Hebrew lessons. However, some Jews did attend the morning service when my father led intercessions for the delegations to the forthcoming San Francisco conference, obviously an exception to normal practice.

Differences

Tensions between those of different faiths were intensified by the proximity in which we lived. Differences of religious outlook, relatively unimportant in normal circumstances, were magnified by the feeling that others, with their annoyingly different ways were too close for co-existence. The tensions were most marked at the outset in 1943 when we were all relatively unknown to one another, for instance the friction between Dr. Chadwick Kew and Mrs. Marco. This occurred over the distribution of foodstuffs received in I.R.C. parcels. Some lively discussion at a camp meeting was followed by strong words from both people, over the best method of sharing the dried fruits and cereals sent to us. The apparent racial friction of their encounter upset 'Skipper' Grant at the time. Probably this was just one example of other similar incidents. [20]

Should the Japanese win our respect for permitting church services to be held regularly, as Norman Cliff suggests? Possibly; according to him, services were allowed on condition that prior notification was given. All meetings of ten or more people needed permission, lest feelings run high, and internees rise up against their guards. Moreover, preachers were to lodge a copy of their sermons with the authorities beforehand. My father's diary makes no reference to this practice. He would have commented on this to my mother, if he had been required to do this; Peter and I would have known. Neither he nor I have any recollection of his submitting a sermon to the Japanese in advance. [21]

Chance conversations could be valuable; my father spent nearly all morning discussing Christianity with two young men, brothers Rodney and Geoffrey Baker. He found himself in similar discussion with Cecil Longhurst, the camp accountant, who had considerable experience of the world prior to internment. He will have been more of a challenge to the missionary personnel, as they explained the roots of their faith, and their reasons for being in China at all. [22]

The friction between those with different beliefs was bound to occur, particularly at that time, before the ecumenical movement was well under way. This was, largely, a post-war development, with the founding of the Church of South India – the first major experiment in formal church unity in 1947, followed by the setting-up of the World Council of Churches in 1948. In one sense Yangchow C was a cradle of ecumenism, as other CAC's will also have been. Inter-church co-operation was largely experimental; Christians and those of other traditions had to play it by the ear of faith.

Mutual tolerance had developed a good deal by 1988, when people of many religious persuasions attended the service at St. George's Chapel, Windsor, during the 1988 "Once in a lifetime" Reunion.

[1] Willis, G. C., *I was among the Captives*. For his view of ordination, see p.73
[2] HFW, 16 April 1943 and 12 June 1943. For the estimate of attendance at Mass, see my father's précis of camp life, *penes* P. R. Wickings.
[3] Keith Martin, unpublished memoir, p.14 and HFW, 18 July 1943
[4] HFW, typewritten account of Yangchow, *penes* PRW. No date, composed after 1945.
[5] All the information about Rev. George Henderson comes from one of his letters, dated 20 August 1945, to a correspondent back home
[6] Father James Thornton, S.J. letter to HFW, 18 October 1990, *penes* PRW
[7] Angus, p.138
[8] HFW, 13 August 1943
[9] For the committee's ban, see HFW, 1 June 1943. Willis' own account is in his book, pp.93-6.
[10] Willis' own account of the Hell debate is in his book, pp.118-9. My father's view in his diary, 1 October 1944
[11] PRW, recollections, June 2002
[12] HFW, *passim*
[13] Begley, *Separated for Service*, p.76; Willis, pp.90-1; HFW, 9 May 1943
[14] Begley family, *Separated for Service*, *passim*, and HFW, *passim*
[15] For Gwen Morris' Chinese classes, see Taylor, P.A., unpublished memoir, p.8. For Betty James' – "a brilliant teacher" – Walford Gillison, recollections, June 2002
[16] HFW, 25 April 1943
[17] A.. B. Linkhorn is mentioned as the only man killed when H.M.S. Peterel was sunk, in Hugh Collar's book *Captive in Shanghai*, p.16. A later account by Bernard Wasserstein gives the figure of six men killed; the total crew was 18. See Wasserstein, B., *Secret War in Shanghai*, pp.97-9.
[18] For the Russian icons and the reference to the Archbishop's visit, I am in debt to Keith Martin, October 2002
[19] Keith Martin, recollections, July 2002. The final point comes from David Bolton's recollections, June 2002
[20] HFW, 20 August 1943
[21] Cliff, *Prisoners of the Samurai*, p.82
[22] HFW, 30 November 1943

PARCELS

One of the great delights of privation is a break from routine. For us in Yangchow C, this meant the arrival of parcels from Shanghai. They contained food, and items that were luxuries, by camp standards: cigarettes; for the men, razors and shaving soap; for the women toiletries such as good soap. Soap became valuable: often one received it as a birthday gift from a friend in camp. Everyone savoured the food: dried milk, called KLIM, liver paté, tinned salmon, Spam – then, if not now – a treat, and coffee. Peter Gibson, then aged 8, remembers:

> "The bliss of eating a piece of chocolate." [1]

Cigarettes became the medium of exchange. Smokers were glad to have them as birthday gifts; one lady, Mrs. Green, received 115 on her birthday in March 1945. Non-smokers bartered them for chocolate, or tinned jam. The jam was the wooden pip variety, with coloured turnip pulp masquerading as raspberries. Still, jam. [2]

The excitement stimulated by the prospect of parcels can be felt, tingling through the pages of Beryl Piper's journal. The parcels' arrival was eagerly anticipated. Sometimes the camp authorities learnt of their despatch from Shanghai, and announced this to us. Hopes were raised, and dashed again, when there was a delay.

The delivery of all parcels was a Red Cross responsibility, to safeguard their status in Japanese eyes. But all parcels did not emanate from the Red Cross. Some were "private", meaning that, prior to internment, internees had arranged for them to be sent at monthly intervals. Hence some people never had private parcels since they had either not known of this plan, or been unable, possibly through lack of funds, to arrange for a neutral in Shanghai to send them. Apart from these, there were genuine I.R.C. parcels, sometimes American, once British, in origin. These were for all internees.

L.M.S. missionaries were among the group who had arranged for monthly parcels. People temporarily housed in the Columbia Country Club, on the outskirts of Shanghai, discussed the scheme: the Swiss Consul General provided a £10 grant for each missionary family. My father spent an entire evening helping B.M.S. and L.M.S. colleagues complete the necessary forms; all over Shanghai other British nationals made similar plans. [3]

When we had been in camp for a month, we began to hope for parcels. But the I.R.C. scheme for delivering them was to begin only when all British and American nationals were interned. Father O'Collins, the first Roman Catholic priest in Yangchow C, arrived exactly a month after we did. People's hopes were disappointed when he stated that some British passport holders in Shanghai were still to be interned. When the first packages did arrive, two days after Easter, my father noted ruefully:

> "Parcels arrived for some people ... but none for us." [4]

Initially we expected the parcels to come at monthly intervals. But like London buses, they "bunched": two or even three months' supply would arrive together. We waited, and waited, and waited again: still they failed to materialise. My father's mischievous sense of humour made him set "Red Cross parcels" as an essay topic for his Vth form English class. Once, by magic it seemed, they came, bang on cue. On Christmas Eve 1943, our first Christmas in camp, the accumulated supply of three months' waiting arrived:

> "All ready for carol service when Sept. Oct. and Nov. parcels arrived (4.45 p.m.). Bustle, noise and chaos till 8.20 – clearing, opening and brushing up. Worthwhile: the camp thrilled." [5]

On one occasion some packages from the British Red Cross were damaged, so their contents were bad and had to be thrown away. Considering all the difficulties of transport, they usually arrived surprisingly intact.

Of course, parcels were welcomed in other camps in similar fashion. At Lunghua, just outside Shanghai, Eleanor Box and her crowd of friends eagerly awaited the lorries, which were visible from a long distance away. Her non-smoking parents traded cigarettes for food so their monotonous diet could be varied, as Mrs. Box baked delicious cakes. [6]

And the men in Haiphong Rd., Hugh Collar and his companions, appreciated the two consignments of parcels they received from the American Red Cross.

> "Whoever made them up showed rare sympathy and understanding of what would most appeal to people long deprived of the ordinary amenities of life ... " [7]

Again, young Rosemary Green's journal shows a long period between her first hearing that parcels were on the way, and their actual arrival. It was intensely cold; records show that Shanghai experienced its coldest winter since 1871, in 1945. Besides the terrible cold, we had been without lighting for much of the time. People had chilblains on their fingers, their toes, their heels. Everyone, young and old, felt the strain of internment.

In mid-March parcels were rumoured to be outside our gates. Next, they were to arrive within a week, the next Monday or Tuesday. By early April, people grew cynical, saying the parcels had not even left Shanghai.

"Needless to say, parcels not here" notes Rosemary in mid-April. She voices the general pessimism:

> "All think parcels are never coming."

We waited throughout May. On 2nd June they finally arrived, to great excitement. But – there was nothing for the Green family. Next day, friends gave them goodies – including jam, salami and bacon. These friends ranged from a Jewish lady, to Protestant missionaries, the Hendersons, whose son was friendly with Rosemary's brother, Leslie. The Greens were Catholics, but by now religious differences were irrelevant. Friends supported you, when life seemed tough. [8]

The contents of American I.R.C. packages were shared by everyone. Rosemary thought it really marvellous when her family received tinned milk, butter, meat, chocolate and chewing gum. By a happy coincidence, it was her father's birthday. Later, Rosemary won some tinned bacon at the canteen tombola. [9]

Would we have survived if there had been no Red Cross parcels? The question is debatable; probably we would have done so. The diet supplied by the Japanese was crude and unpalatable, but we did not receive the meagre amounts on which some Prisoners of War existed – those on the Burma railroad or in Taiwan. In the camps described so graphically by Arthur Titherington and Jack Edwards, men were doing heavy manual labour; many of them endured and survived. At our release we were undoubtedly thin and some people seriously underweight. Some had long-term health problems which could be traced to internment. But there were vitamins in the scanty bowls of vegetable stew. Colin Palmer, having qualified as a doctor in the years immediately after 1945, states:

> "In retrospect, we had adequate amounts of B group vitamins (the bread, cracked wheat and unpolished rice), Vitamin C in potatoes and root vegetables, some A and D in the pork fat [each family had a ration of lard issued at irregular intervals – Author] and of course Vitamin D from the sunshine." [10]

A fair conclusion may well be that we emerged from Yangchow in relatively better shape than many POWs; this was, in part, due to the parcels we received.

Of course both at the time, and later, some people believed the parcels were essential to our survival. My father was only voicing an opinion held by many, when he wrote:

> "Don't know what we should do without Red Cross parcels." [11]

In October 1945, W. H. Taylor, a former Yangchow internee, stated that Mr. V. Smith had died in January of the same year for lack of sufficient proper food. His statement later appeared as evidence when, in 1947, Commandant Hashizumi, and N.C.O. Tanaka were investigated for war crimes. Other internees, whose evidence was also used in these investigations, clearly thought the parcels were necessary to our well-being.

Moreover, their evidence included complaints that the Japanese stole both food and cigarettes from Red Cross packages. This is supported by the recollections of many former internees. Beryl Evelyn Smith, an employee of Sassoons after the war, was regarded by the Allied military authorities as a reliable witness. Her testimony, in February 1947, was that Commandant Hashizumi only allowed 50% of the parcels to be distributed; the remainder were to be kept as iron rations. When internees disregarded this edict, and issued all the parcels, Hashizumi cut the normal rations by half, saying we could feed ourselves from the parcels' contents. This related to June 1945; by then the Japanese were short of food supplies themselves.

The pilfering of cigarettes was a particularly sore point. Alf Read stated, also in October 1945, that the Japanese guards stole American cigarettes, and smoked them before we internees could do so. [12]

Razors from the U.S.A. were also coveted by the guards, as the following tale shows. Mr. W. G. Bown had set up a small workshop where he mended watches, clocks and other small items. One of the guards brought him a broken American razor, to be mended, with the words:

"This no go. You fix."

"I suggest you take it back to the shop where you bought it" came Bown's swift retort. [13]

Certainly the arrival of parcels created a mood of elation among us. Obviously it would have been preferable for them to reach us at monthly intervals. It was war-time; we were fortunate that they reached us at all, so far from Shanghai. Their sporadic arrival and the build-up of tension which preceded their entry to camp made a break in the tedious camp routine. The downside was the disruption caused when the parcels actually came, disruption in terms of unpacking, the absence of young people from school classes – always a source of irritation to their teachers, the dirt, noise and general confusion. But no-one would have been without the parcels. Probably their psychological value was at least as great as their contents. The world had not forgotten us – even if parcels were always late, and the letters we sent did not reach their destinations. Days when the parcels came were the highlights of camp life. Fay Westwood called them "golden days". To change the metaphor, Red Cross parcels provided red letter occasions. [14]

1. Peter Gibson, recollections, September 2002
2. Rosemary Green, 13 March 1945
3. HFW, 18 February 1943. Compare Geoffrey L. Gale, *Interned in China*, p.16
4. HFW, entries for 15, 16, 18 and 27 April 1943
5. HFW, 24 December 1943
6. Phyllis and Eleanor Box, recollections, June 2002
7. Collar, *Captive in Shanghai*, p.116
8. Rosemary Green, successive diary entries, 19 March to 3 June 1945
9. Rosemary Green, diary 4 and 6 June 1945
10. Colin Palmer, recollections, December 2002
11. HFW, 24 June 1945
12. WO 325, 122, P.R.O.
13. Keith Martin, recollections, September 2002
14. Angus, p.120

ISOLATION

"Mum, Mum, why are we standing for so long?"

I tugged at the hem of my mother's skirt, as we stood at roll call, one morning in April 1945.

"Hush, Grace, hush! A great man has died."

Franklin Roosevelt died on April 12th; less than a fortnight later, we accorded him two minutes' respectful silence. Shortly after, my father recorded Vice-President Truman's succession to the White House. [1]

About the same time, my father led the camp's Protestants in intercession for the delegates to the San Francisco Conference, at the usual Sunday morning service. There was a full congregation, with even some of the Jewish community present. So we, apparently cut off in remote Yangchow, knew of the free world's attempt at establishing a forum to settle world problems, the United Nations. [2]

How then did we learn of events in the world beyond the confining camp walls? Letters were no use in this respect; with strict censorship they could contain no political or military news. We had three sources of information, one through the newspaper, *The Shanghai Times*. Next, people were occasionally allowed to visit Shanghai, for some form of medical treatment. Then, the Chinese coming into the camp, usually the Glamour Girls, might impart the news for which the adults longed so much. And yet we did learn of the major events – albeit some time after they happened: the fall of Italy, D-Day, the attempt on Hitler's life. We knew less about the progress of war in the Pacific but the presence of increasing numbers of U.S. aircraft in the sky was an encouraging sign.

But there were always rumours, often of our impending departure from Yangchow.

One of the most difficult problems was to disentangle genuine news from rumours – whether of events in Europe, or of developments which could affect us directly. The most pressing of these was possible repatriation. This was particularly relevant at the time when Camps A and B moved down to Shanghai, in September 1943. My father was apprehensive that we in Yangchow C might go too, and find ourselves in conditions inferior to those we were starting to know in our town on the Grand Canal.

> "Heard we are definitely going from Mr. Grant, at the end of the month. Hope it is to be repatriated.."

So wrote Beryl Piper. Mothers aired bedding before packing it into bundles. But ten days later, our Camp Representative announced we would remain at Yangchow for the coming winter, and not move elsewhere. [3]

Rosemary Green's journal recorded similar rumours before the Belgians came, in the six-week period before their arrival, on 16 November 1944.

The Shanghai Times

This was the only newspaper to arrive at Yangchow; its news items were subject to heavy Japanese censorship. Walford Gillison remembers mocking references to the British Navy as a "rubber navy", whenever the paper reported a British naval defeat. The Japanese did not censor reports of German or Fascist Italy defeats by the Allies. But they were reluctant to allow publication of their own defeats, by land or sea. We internees could read between the lines:

> "[The paper] was put up on the notice board ... I used to look up in an atlas where the fighting had reached in the

Pacific, or North Africa, or in Russia, or, after D-Day, in France. Thus, although the Allied fleets had been sunk many times over, and their armies defeated over and over again, one could see on the map the war getting even closer to Germany and Japan." [4]

Radio News

All personal radios had been confiscated prior to internment; hence we felt the lack of its immediate news acutely. Keith Gillison felt that we were fortunate in having none, since mere possession of a radio could mean death. Colin and Edith Begley, previously in Stanley camp, Hong Kong, told of the shooting of one man who had smuggled a radio in, together with nine other internees, selected apparently at random, who suffered the same fate. [5]

However, we did occasionally hear odd snippets of news via the radio used by our guards. Their radio was prone to frequent breakdowns. An ex-wireless operator, who was one of our internees, offered his services to repair it.

> "Needless to say, the breakdown took all day to fix; during this time, the operator picked items of exciting news." [6]

So in various ways we did come to know of the major developments of the great conflict in Europe. Admittedly, this was always late; it was not until July and August 1945 that we felt really cut off as the American advance in the Pacific brought the end of the war close to Yangchow.

Two European developments have been chosen to show how long it took for us to learn of them; they are the D-Day landings, and the bomb-plot against Hitler's life. D-Day itself was 6th June 1944. The excitement of this second front is reflected in the writing of Beryl Piper. She wrote:

> "Landed in France – Marvellous news ... We have advanced into France: Dieppe, Dunkirk and have captured Calais."

> "We have walked into Brussels."

These entries were made on successive days. By now, some young men were able to elude the guards, with ease.

> "Last night, Buzzy (nickname for Lancelot Wade) went over the wall ... a dare, silly fool." [7]

My father commented in similar mood; he had – earlier on – speculated on the weather, and its favourability to Churchill's enterprise.

Closer to home, Beryl faced her School Certificate exams and so her journal interpolates the Normandy news with notes of revision for maths or history. Ironically, my father was the person who both set and marked the same history scripts.

The Stauffenberg Bomb Plot, July 1944

The attempted assassination of Hitler, and its failure, appears in Beryl Piper's journal:

> "Some German soldiers tried to kill Hitler but unfortunately were caught in time."

My father's version added a note on the departure of the Tojo Cabinet in Japan, and its replacement. He continued:

> "Both these items significant. Amer(icans) landed on Guam."

It took more than a week for the news of Claus von Stauffenberg's bomb to reach us. As for the Pacific, he and his friends guessed that Japan faced increasing threats as Allied forces advanced. [8]

Letters

We were almost entirely deprived of letters, like other civilian internees. We could only write if we used the standard Red Cross pro forma, which limited one's message to 25 words; it had to be news of a personal nature. It took considerable ingenuity to compress family news into such a short space. We were restricted to one letter each month. The reverse side of the pro forma allowed the recipient to write a reply. We have two examples of I.R.C. letters, showing the Japanese censor's stamp. They reached England via Cairo and Ankara. Of course it all took time. My brother's painstaking pencil sent Christmas greetings to my aunt in Newcastle-upon-Tyne; it was dated 28th August 1944. The letter cannot have reached her till well into the New Year, since Ankara is date-stamped 22nd January 1945, while her reply, on the reverse, was written on 5th April.

Some letters never reached their destination. In December 1944 Dad received a letter from his sister, Doreen, in which she seemed quite unaware of our being interned. Her letter had taken eleven months to reach us; obviously some correspondence had gone astray. Indeed we were fortunate to have heard from England at all. After liberation the British Captain Martin, who became responsible for our camp, found more than 100 letters for us internees in the Japanese commandant's desk. [9]

Occasionally the authorities made exceptions to the rules about letters, as when my father learned of the death of Dorothy Robjohns, wife to an L.M.S. colleague from Australia, Dr. Collin Robjohns. He wrote:

> " ... a terrible blow for Collin and the children. Am trying to get Grant to induce Hashizumi to allow me to send letter of sympathy."

And the following day:

> "Hashizumi has consented to letter going to Robbie: good."

What is not clear about this sad little episode, which reflects well on Commandant Hashizumi, and on Grant, the camp representative, is how my father learnt of Dorothy's death at all. [10]

Some people were understandably anxious about their sons or husbands serving in the armed forces. The Red Cross had the melancholy task of relaying the news of death in combat. Mr. Grant gave Arthur Piper a telegram; it read:

> "Break gently to Arthur L. Piper 12/1 Camp C quote "News of son's gallant death abroad in May" unquote. (Ref. No. 935 B 307). Signed Ed Egle."

And my father's version:

> "Piper has heard his only son killed. Roe ditto. Losses terrible to think about on both sides, and all for what?" [11]

On a less sombre note, Scottish Mrs. Jessie Ferguson, one of Yangchow's unattached ladies, or "loose women", as the Japanese so delightfully referred to them, was chatting to Mrs. Jewell, known to her friends as "Brownie", one day. She had no idea of the whereabouts of her husband Dougie, a naval engineer; she confided that, having no news of him, she had written a letter, which ran thus:

"Dougie, are you alive or dead? Where the hell are you?" I wonder whether she despatched this missive, and, if so, where she addressed it, possibly care of Jardine Matheson, Dougie's employers, or even to Hell itself. [12]

Such letters as did get through created an enormous sense of relief among those receiving them. To know one's family had survived the London blitz, or other enemy action, was obviously heartening, even if details could not be conveyed in a mere 25 words.

Of course, once we were liberated and were permitted to send proper letters, unhindered as to length, and best of all, free of charge, people expressed their feelings as fully as they wished. The cache of letters written by Chris Willis, and his wife Jean, was discovered by their grand-daughter, Hope Hambly. They relate to early September 1945, when Jean and her husband were rejoicing in the freedom to write to sons and daughters in Canada, telling how our life had changed since our liberation. The letters are full of love and longing, though the world beyond Yangchow still seemed infinitely remote:

"Darling little Hope" was their newly arrived grand-daughter; Chris was able to congratulate his daughter on her birth. By the time he wrote this, the couple had received seven letters, from other friends and relatives. This was the first real news they had had for over a year. One of Jean's letters is particularly touching. She describes the new clothes which Chris had been given by the Red Cross. And tells of her own careful saving of a green costume, carefully packed away from the depredations of moths and mice:

> " ... and I've Fanny's green hat to match. I have kept them in reserve to go home in."

- a typically feminine ploy even in internment camp conditions. After so many months of pent-up emotion, Jean's letter ends:

> "You know I can never write all that is in my heart." [13]

Apart from these obvious interruptions to our isolation, some survivors can recall isolated sounds of the outside world. Among these were the burst of gunfire, usually at night, as Chinese guerrillas took on the Japanese in Yangchow city. And often a monastery bell boomed to mark Buddhist prayer times.

The last two months of the war was the time when we felt most isolated. All the journals reflect the knowledge that Japan must soon acknowledge defeat.

> "Japan being bombed unmercifully. How long can she hold?"

We could, of course, both see and hear the American bombers pass overhead. Meanwhile camp life continued its normal pattern; P. C. Matthews, together with other senior teachers, my father among them, were interviewing the parents of the older students about possible future careers. Vocational classes in accountancy and secretarial skills went on, as we began to learn details of Attlee's Labour landslide. [14]

Then, at last, the bombshell:

> "It is said in the local Chinese papers that the war has stopped ... hard to say what is happening."

Further:

> "Puzzled that no official word given as to the political situation ... Why doesn't an Allied plane drop a message? We are a lost legion!" [15]

Of course, we children cared little for the adults' bewilderment; it meant nothing to us, so we could not share their dreadful sense of being left out of the world events which had swept us into internment.

Beryl Piper learnt the news in different fashion:

> "A guard told Lamb in his room: THE WAR IS OVER. I think it must be true."

Yamamoto, the little roly-poly guard, so often the butt of our teasing, was in tears when he told "Buzzy" Wade that it was all over. And so, in such casual fashion, we learnt of impending liberation. [16]

---

[1] HFW, 15 April; Beryl Piper, 23 April; also HFW 26 April; all entries in 1945
[2] HFW, 22 April 1945
[3] Beryl Piper, 6 October; HFW and Beryl Piper entries for 19 October. All dates in 1943.
[4] Walford Gillison, recollection, June 2002 and Peter Gibson, recollections, September 2002
[5] Keith Gillison, *The Cross and The Dragon*, p.165
[6] Hudson Felgate, unpublished memoir, 1994, p.4
[7] Beryl Piper, entries for 9, 10 and 11 June 1944
[8] Beryl Piper, and HFW, 28 July 1944
[9] HFW, 9 December, and Willis, p.132
[10] HFW, 4 and 5 April 1944
[11] Beryl Piper, and HFW, 11 September 1944
[12] Story from Mrs. G. L. Jewell, via Keith Martin, her nephew, September 2002
[13] Chris Willis letter, 30 September 1945, and Jean Willis, letter to Hope, her daughter, 9 September 1945
[14] HFW, 16 July 1945
[15] HFW, 15 August 1945
[16] Beryl Piper, 15 August 1945

JAPANESE

Many people know little of the events in the Far East which led up to Japan's entry into World War II. The image of Japanese guards is one of cruelty to their captives. Many people think of films – *Bridge on the River Kwai* and *Empire of the Sun*. They know of the Japanese military code: absolute obedience to the Emperor, which bade the soldiers prefer suicide, to the humiliation of surrender. "How dreadful was it for you?" enquirers ask those of us interned in camps in China.

Such people are aware of Japan's invasion of Manchuria in 1931, and also of the attack on Pearl Harbour, more than ten years later, in December 1941. The intervening decade is something of a blank. Sufficient to say that Japanese hunger to expand well beyond the confines of their islands had begun long before 1900 and to Korea in 1910. The Sino-Japanese war was triggered by the incident at the Marco Polo bridge just outside Peking, in July 1937. From then on Westerners might learn of the horrors inflicted on the Chinese, especially of the rape of Nanking, when thousands of Chinese were massacred, sick people in hospital thrown out of the window into the street below, and so many Chinese women were violated. [1]

As for the international city of Shanghai itself, the Japanese attack by land, sea and air began in August 1937. It took four months, according to Dr. Stephen Sturton, for the Imperial Army to establish control of the city. Meantime Dr. Sturton was caring for the most badly wounded of the Chinese troops in the C.M.S. hospital at Hongkew, south of Shanghai. By November 1937 he was receiving regular financial help for the hospital from the Lord Mayor of London's fund for Relief in China. [2]

Most adults in Yangchow will have known of the massacres at Nanking. They will also have heard the stories of Bridge House and Haiphong Rd., camps in Shanghai – closer to home for most of them. Here Japanese interrogators tried to elicit information from the men imprisoned in these two camps; there is no need for me to describe the tortures inflicted there. Hugh Collar and Norman Cliff have already done so. [3]

Our experience was less severe. It was always possible that harsh treatment would be meted out to those who broke, or who appeared to break, the rules imposed by Japanese authority:

> "As long as we did exactly as the Japanese commandant instructed us, we were not physically mistreated. Some, who did not obey, were taken to the guardhouse, where they were punished." [4]

Punishment could be a slap across the face; for more serious offences people were forced to stand or kneel for long periods, as the following incident shows.

Hudson Felgate, then aged twenty, came in for punishment when he purloined two sheets of corrugated iron to make a shelter for those stoking the hospital fire. R. K. Stott – a dour Cornish sea-captain – known as "Don" Stott – was Hudson's accomplice. Stoking the hospital furnace was a smoky task; it was especially stressful in summer heat. Stokers needed shelter from the blazing sun, and the torrential downpour of Yangchow thunderstorms. One night, Don Stott and Hudson took two corrugated iron sheets from their resting-place near the guardhouse, and hid them, intending to make a shelter. But next day at roll call, the authorities announced the theft, and demanded the culprits own up. If they did not, the entire parade would remain standing all day and all night. Guards fixed their bayonets in position.

Hudson and Don could do nothing but confess; they marched out in front of the commandant. The culprits had to bring the hidden sheets to the parade ground; then they had to carry them between the lines of their fellow campers. Up and down, up and down they went. After returning the stolen iron to the guardhouse, the two men had to stand all day, while guards shouted at them. Both fully expected to be shot; in fact, they were allowed home at the end of the day. In their church billet, Hudson's mother lay prostrate on her bed: the victim of a minor heart attack. [5]

Many factors explain the relative moderation of Japanese behaviour to us.

First, many of those whose memories contribute to this account, were young children at the time; our parents shielded us from horrors as best they could. Others – Marjorie Train, Keith Martin, Owen Manley and Peggy Taylor, for instance – were teenagers, or in their early twenties. They recall more detail, and sometimes harsher incidents than those about my own age, simply because of the ten or twelve years' age gap. My brother, David Bolton, Peter Gibson and I were younger and so, more protected.

Further, many "Japanese" patrolling the compound and supervising roll calls were actually Korean peasants. They too were expatriates in hostile surroundings. Many had children of their own, and will have missed them while they served in China. When I, my brother, Walford Gillison and David Bolton recall some smiling guards, our memories do not play us false. Kick the can was the great game for summer evenings, alternating with hide and seek. We sped over the grass, to approach the "right" guard, who could be wheedled into delaying the curfew for another five, or even ten minutes. Some guards allowed the boys to play with their swords, though never with their revolvers. [6]

The Japanese could not afford to be overly harsh: they needed our medical skills. The classic account of a missionary surgeon's removal of an inflamed appendix from a Japanese guard appears in full elsewhere in this account. Again, Dr. Gell and Matron Wheal delivered the first child of Tanera, who had returned from his wedding leave shortly before.[7]

The guards might want to improve their languages – the Boltons taught English to a "Mr. G." Another guard secured a certificate declaring him unfit for military service from Dr. Bolton. One or two guards were Christians, attending Willis' Gospel sessions:

"Some of the guards were ready to be friendly" wrote Willis. But fraternisation was forbidden, at least in theory.[8]

Roll Calls

The most obvious sign of Japanese authority was the morning roll call, outside on the parade ground. We stood in groups of about 50 people, to be counted. Each group had a leader; the leaders were known to us all as "the blockheads". The guards checked to see no-one had escaped. At first, the count was done in English. When this proved ineffective, we were told to learn Japanese numerals. Those in camp with some knowledge of Japanese, Mr. Gray and Mrs. Piper among them, taught the rest of us. As children, we picked up the numbers swiftly. We enjoyed chanting "ichi, nee, san, shee, go" and so on. Indeed the boys took a peculiar delight in shouting "Go" very loudly to the guards. They would wriggle themselves into position five, fifteen or twenty-five, in the long line, just to be able to shout it. But some adults found learning Japanese difficult. One person always had to be in the 25th position. The only number which stuck in his memory was

"Ni ju go – Need you go?"

Ian Mackinnon recollects that the Willis family found the Japanese numbers difficult.[9]

At the outset, roll call could take more than half an hour; with time the guards became more competent. A few people were always unwell, either in hospital, or confined to their own beds. Some individuals – often the engineers – might be engaged on some vital camp task. Evening roll call took place in our accommodation blocks.

At Lunghua, roll call was always held outside internees' rooms. Lateness was an offence. On one occasion Jowett Murray, an L.M.S. colleague of my parents, failed to rouse his children from their beds in time for evening roll call. The guard used the scabbard of his sword to inflict a few blows. [10]

The long periods of standing in line were hard to bear in the great summer heat. Women fainted and had to be restored. Indeed, the headmaster, Rev. P. C. Matthews, collapsed at roll call, apparently from exhaustion. The roll call was the final straw. [11]

To move while we were standing on parade was an offence, which merited punishment. Van Beynon recalls her father being slapped hard across the face simply because he moved on roll call. Van felt a mixture of anger, helplessness and surprise as she stood next door to her father:

> "I suddenly realised I was capable of killing."

But it was the guard's turn to be surprised when he showed up at the small hole in the wall which served as the pharmacy. He needed medicine for some minor ailment. O. G. R. Beynon confessed feeling a strong desire to provide the guard with an emetic. [12]

Winter roll calls were infinitely worse, owing to the intense cold; this was particularly so in the winter of 1944-45, when the weather was extremely cold.

> "In the heart of winter snow was shovelled in long furrows to allow the internees to stand, sometimes for an hour or more, until the guards were satisfied there had been no escapes." [13]

Fay Westwood graphically describes her fear of the cold, during roll calls at night. Further, the Japanese reinforced their authority by calling supplementary roll calls. Only a month or so after our arrival at Yangchow, two parades were held in a single morning. The second was held so we could salute a new Japanese CO. [14]

Regular roll calls did achieve their aim: there were no escapes from Yangchow. Possibly no-one felt the urge to escape. We were, after all, civilians, not soldiers or naval personnel, so we were free from the obligation incumbent on all fighting men to elude the patrols and return to carry on the war struggle. A few of our young men did make it over the wall, just to prove the point: it was possible to elude the guards. Certainly they were not the most intelligent of mortals:

> "No army anywhere uses its crème de la crème to guard prison camps." [15]

L. P. Quincey made regular forays over the wall to visit his Chinese contact in the city. He was returning one evening from one of these escapades, when he met Betty James, a chance encounter as she was on an evening stroll round the perimeter fence. After initial alarm, Betty swiftly recovered her poise. From then on, she shared her meagre bread ration with Quincey. He usually met a Yangchow guerrilla who knew the old song *Auld Lang Syne*; they established contact when one of them whistled the first two bars of the tune. The other would respond with the second two bars. [16]

If anyone had succeeded in escaping, life outside camp would have been difficult in the extreme. He would have needed fluent command of the local Chinese dialect. Moreover, the difference in physique between Westerners and the Chinese is so striking that his presence anywhere between Yangchow and Chungking in Free China would have been obvious.

At Yangchow the adults reconciled themselves to sitting out the war. Many people will have discussed the questions my father raised in his diary:

In the autumn of 1944
>"Wonder why the German people don't sue for peace"

and later, in the spring of 1945
>"… Allies have big moves against Japan. Will she capitulate?" [17]

Meantime, regular roll calls continued, as the tense affairs they always had been. However enlightened our Commandant may have been, Yangchow never had the relaxed atmosphere of the camp at Temple Hill, in North China, under the friendly command of Commandant Kosaka. Our rolls calls continued well past VJ Day, on 15th August; the last parade took place five days later. [18]

Misunderstandings

Sometimes the Japanese reacted toughly, from sheer ignorance, as the following incident shows. One evening a Chinese electrician was brought into our cubicle, in the church, to repair a faulty light. When he had finished, my father thanked him in Chinese, saying "Hsieh-hsieh" with a bow, as was customary. Saying thank-you broke the rule: we were not to speak to the Chinese. Dad found himself in the guardroom, until the matter was cleared up. Having lived with a good deal of Japanese bluster, first in Siaokan in 1940/1 and later, in Hankow, Dad was fairly used to questioning. At Siaokan, Japanese officers would question him at night, trying to intimidate him. In this case, at Yangchow, he received an apology from the Japanese guard, the day after the incident. [19]

Similarly, elderly Jesse Gray found guards interrupting his lecture on Kamchatka. By some administrative error, notice that he was giving the lecture had not been posted on the bulletin board. After some tough talk,

Gray had to stop his lecture. Three witnesses, W. J. Bown, Vyvyan Dent and my father, who had been acting as chairman, were required to submit a written account of the incident. My father, who respected Gray's excellent command of the Japanese language, sympathised with his chronic heart condition:

"Old Gray done up – sorry for him." [20]

The embargo on conversation with the Chinese was reinforced when one of the Glamour girls who removed the ordure from the latrines was severely beaten. She was suspected of conveying war news to the internee to whom she spoke. Then the amah had to kneel for long hours in the snow, so all could see. [21]

The Savage Incident

The same punishment was inflicted on Mr. Savage, head of the camp Public Works Department, father to Dennis, Mary and Gordon. Savage was instructed to convert the bath-house into billets for the Belgians; these people were to join Yangchow in mid-November 1944. He had to remove shower cubicles, piping and doors. Savage received permission from the Commandant to transfer two doors, to create an area of privacy in the women's toilets. However, Tanaka, the official supply officer, was not notified. Known as "a beast" for his harsh temper, Tanaka forced Mr. Savage to kneel on the frozen ground outside the guardhouse for 2½ hours.

We children of the church were fascinated. We could see Savage's figure as he knelt alone among the drifting snowflakes. "Come away from that window!" came the curt voice of anxious parents.

The incident proved fortunate for everyone in camp, apart from the Savage family. Grant, Camp Representative, protested to the Japanese authorities. When they refused to listen, he resigned as a matter of principle. The entire camp was in an uproar. Eventually an apology was made, on the advice of an older Japanese guard. Grant resumed his position, and Tanaka left Yangchow, in a matter of weeks.

As for Mr. Savage, to this day, his family marvel that he did not catch pneumonia, though he had suffered a severe attack of malaria three days before the incident. Apparently one knee troubled him in later life. As a dedicated evangelical Christian he had used the time for prayer; others, too, had prayed to support him through the ordeal. [22]

The Savage incident figures largely in charges brought against Tanaka after the war. These charges, alleging cruelty to civilian internees, were investigated by ALFSEA, the Allied Land Forces South East Asia, in February and March 1947. The investigations concluded there was insufficient evidence to bring Tanaka and Commandant Hashizumi to trial for war crimes.

Nonetheless nine Westerners – including one Belgian – alleged that Tanaka had ill-treated internees. Eight witnesses came from Yangchow C; only one relates to Yu Yuen Rd., where Tanaka served before coming to Yangchow. The ill-treatment at Yangchow consisted in Tanaka's method of taking roll call. In the heat of summer, he insisted on prisoners standing for a full 30 minutes in blazing sun. Other guards allowed roll call to be held in the shade of nearby trees. Any moves by children or elderly people when standing in line were enough to make Tanaka increase the time for that particular group to stand to attention. [23]

Tanaka is fully described in these investigations, as an NCO in the Japanese Consular Police. Aged about 32, 5 feet 4 inches tall and c.105 lbs. in weight, he was slim, sallow-skinned, clean-shaven, with close-cropped hair. Well-groomed and without glasses, he spoke fluent Mandarin. Unlike Hashizumi, he was not in Allied custody in March 1947. Maybe he was never captured; maybe he died before this time. Possibly he had quietly returned home.

One Yangchow witness, R. K. Stott, singled out Tanaka, terming him "arrogant". W. A. Macdonald's account of the Savage incident relates that Tanaka slapped the face of Savage's son, when he brought his father's coat, hat and gloves, as protection against the severe weather. Beryl Smith's testimony states that Mr. Savage was only released because of the intervention of camp doctors, who insisted that Savage was confined to bed for two or three days afterwards. [24]

As for Tanaka, it was fortunate for him that he did leave. Some of the men had sworn to revenge themselves on him, given the opportunity at the end of the war.

> "Tanaka, who had been particularly vicious, would be singled out for harshest revenge."

Hashizumi attempted to defend Tanaka: he shifted responsibility to his deputy, Tamura. Before this incident Tanaka had been, in the Commandant's own words, "well-behaved". Most people at Yangchow would not agree, as the written testimonies show. [25] [26]

The final disposition

Some survivors from Yangchow C believe the Japanese planned to shoot us all, when the war ended. Allied officers apparently found orders for our extermination in the headquarters in early September 1945. Others find this idea incredible, arguing that the Japanese would surely have destroyed such orders, rather than let them fall into Allied hands.

Conversely, allowing orders for the extermination of civilians to be discovered, while we had obviously survived, can be seen as one way for the Japanese to save their skins. A shrewd Japanese might calculate that defiance of orders from higher authority could benefit guards in the eyes of the Allies. Such defiance might signify a measure of humanity.

What of other civilian camps? According to Norman Cliff, extermination of civilians was planned at Lunghua. Cliff quotes Arthur Clarke:

> "Peace came just in time … It is said documents were discovered proving the Japanese had planned to exterminate civilian internees in groups, owing to the increased difficulty of feeding us, also as a reprisal for the bombing of Japanese cities." [27]

As for Fengtai, where Hugh Collar and his fellows from Haiphong Rd. had been moved, under later interrogation Lieutenant Honda stated that he had discussed with fellow guards whether they should kill all the prisoners and then commit hara-kiri themselves. [28]

As for the Shanghai camps, George Scott, writing in 1946, stated:

> "It was learned later that by so narrow a margin as five days Shanghai had been spared the horrors of invasion. A member of the American Military Mission … stated that August 15th was the date fixed for a major landing north and south of the city." [29]

In such a situation Japanese guards at the civilian camps might well have killed their prisoners, before committing suicide themselves.

None of this is conclusive evidence for plans against us at Yangchow C. Yet there is some evidence to support the view that the guards at least contemplated our extermination. Two drawings, made by S. J. Smith, exist of a building on the city wall. The first, dated 1943, shows a derelict pillbox. The second, dated 1945, shows the same building, roofed, with five portholes, probably for machine guns in position to fire into the camp. Further, my father records:

> "Some fortifications, of a sort, being made upon the city wall here."

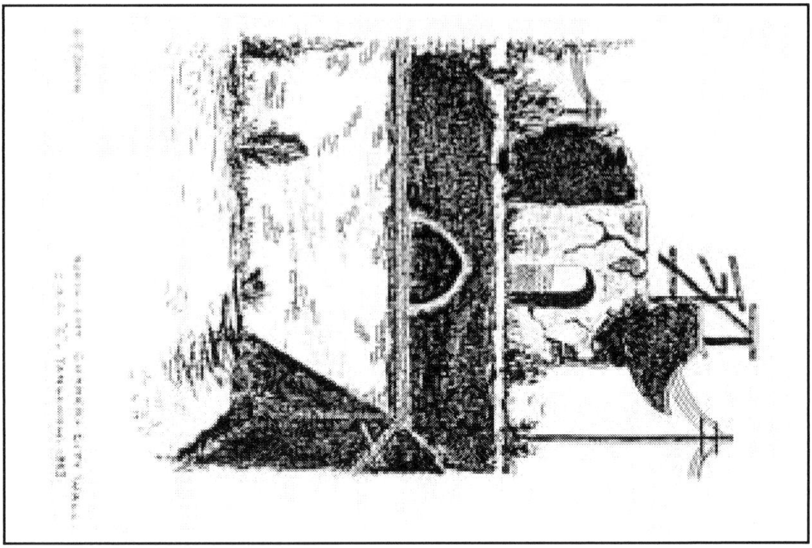

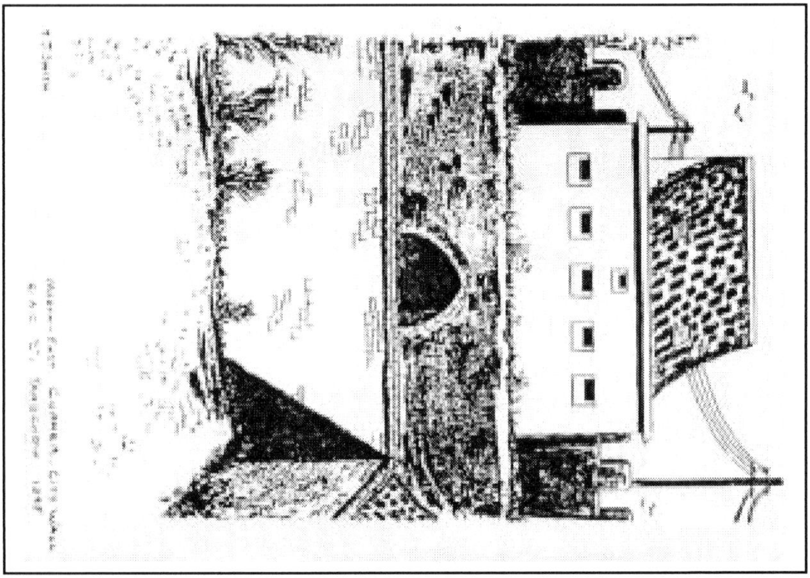

One can only suppose that the diary entry refers to the newly constructed building of S. J. Smith's sketches, and that the Japanese authorities were taking precautions against a possible rising of internees.

Whatever the significance of these developments, a story still circulates among survivors that the guards feared a body of our men would rush the guardhouse and overpower our captors, if we knew the war was over. Apparently Grant, our leader, reassured the commandant that we had one wish and only one: to go home. The story is characteristic of Grant, and of the moderation which had led to the comparative good relations between the Japanese and those of us interned in Yangchow C; it has the ring of truth.

> "Dispose of them as the situation dictates ... whether by bombing, poisons, drowning, decapitation or what ... Annihilate them all ..."

This extreme measure for the disposal of POWs in Japanese hands must be understood in context. The document, from which I have just quoted, is an entry from the journal of the POW Camp HQ at Taihoku in Taiwan, dated 1st August 1944. The full text reads:

> "The time and method of this disposition are as follows:
>
> 1) <u>The time</u> ... individual disposition may be made in the following circumstances:
>   a) when an uprising of large numbers cannot be suppressed without the use of firearms
>   b) when escapees from the camp may turn into a hostile fighting force
>
> 2) <u>The methods</u>
>   a) Whether they are destroyed individually or in groups or however it is done, with mass bombing, poisonous smoke, poisons,

> drowning, decapitation or what, dispose of them as the situation dictates.
> b) In any case, it is the aim not to allow the escape of a single one, to annihilate them all, and not leave any traces."

This document 2701 – certified as Exhibit "O" in Document No. 2687 – emanates from the International Prosecution Section: British Division. It was cited as evidence at the war crimes trials in Hong Kong.

Is it relevant to the last months we spent at Yangchow C in the summer of 1945? Terrifying as its proposals are for the final disposition of POWs, one cannot argue that this disposition would have been applied to us. Firstly, the document relates to military camps, such as Kinkaseki, in Taiwan, rather than to civilian camps in mainland China, as Yangchow C was. Further, the final disposition was a response to a hypothetical question "What should a Japanese commandant do in the case of a mass rising against his authority?" And this situation never arose in our camp.

To summarise, two attitudes towards the Japanese prevailed in 1945. The first, expressed by George Henderson, was gentle; to Henderson we had experienced little cruelty worth the recording. This was probably a minority view. The second was the majority view, expressed with most clarity by Beryl Smith in the preliminary hearings for a war crimes trial against Hashizumi and Tanaka. This attitude was harsher; it detailed the inhumane treatment we experienced, notably inadequate food, the stealing from such International Red Cross supplies we did receive, and finally accommodation, which was quite inappropriate for the many women and children, especially that provided for the 38 Belgians.

The Guards

Dark navy blue was the colour worn by our guards; the uniform colour was so dark it seemed almost black. Each guard had a Mauser pistol. Their swords were not the long Samurai type; they were short, like

Yangchow Years

European ceremonial swords, with silver scabbards polished to a high gloss. These short swords were carried by all ranks, except officers. They had Samurai swords, reserved for officers like Colonel Nishida, and for the senior NCOs. [30]

One or two individuals stand out. Yamamoto was a cheerful roly-poly chap, proud of his wife and family. Scruffy in appearance, trousers held in position by strings of white tape, never a belt, short in the leg and so forever in danger of tripping over his giant sword. At roll call, bold females would tease him. He would try to flee from one set of smiles by a retreat to the next line of feminine ogling. His head was shaved, to add to the incongruity of this comic figure. Despite the rule against fraternisation, Yamamoto tried to talk to the young lads, though his English was scanty, and their Japanese was non-existent. If Japan was defeated, would he have to commit hara-kiri? Neil Begley envisaged

> "little Yamamoto kneeling … and plunging a large knife deep into his pudgy stomach" [31]

"Big Sword" was the nickname given to Colonel Nishida, second in command of our camp for some of the time. Nishida liked to demonstrate his authority by insisting we stood to attention, in silence, during roll call. "At ease! Attention!" Twice more the commands were barked out, before we were dismissed. Possibly this was a reprisal, since just before Ronnie Laycock, aged 18, had been taken to the guardhouse, only because a guard suspected Ronnie had been mocking him. Possibly by this time, summer 1945, the Japanese were increasingly sensitive to mockery, since Japan clearly faced imminent defeat. [32]

Yamashita was the first of the two commandants at Yangchow. People remember him as a tough individual from the severe tone of his initial harangue to us when we arrived. Moreover, each adult had to promise to make no complaint about the food or accommodation provided for us. Yamashita controlled all three Yangchow camps, until A and B closed, in September 1943. It is tempting to identify Yamashita with the tough

Japanese of the same name who replaced a fairly reasonable commandant at Lunghua, under whose command several internees had escaped. Yamashita was followed at Yangchow by Hashizumi, who remained in charge till our liberation. [33]

Hashizumi was a reasonable, fair-minded person. We were fortunate that he had himself been interned in Allied camps earlier in the war, and had been impressed with the way he had been treated. His sympathy with our plight was shown in a number of ways: for instance, his encouragement of our growing vegetables in the camp gardens, and his presentation of prizes and certificates at school Speech Days. He approved the digging of the new well, to improve our water-supply; of course, it was beneficial for his guards too. Further, Hashizumi showed his understanding of Keith Martin when Keith decided to stay at Yangchow, in preference to going, with his sister June, to Hong Kong, as both would further their education by staying. [34]

The Japanese attitude to animals showed their latent cruelty. Some guards beat a dog to death with iron bars. They would trap the bulbuls for food; tiny birds, even smaller than sparrows, which the guards caught in fowlers' nets or shot. We prisoners were not the only ones facing starvation; so too were our guards. [35]

Japanese cruelty was most obvious in the way they regarded and treated the Chinese. They seem to have had some respect for Westerners; Hugh Collar records the Japanese naval officer who sank H.M.S. Peterel, expressing his deep admiration for the bravery with which Lieut. Stephen Polkinghorn and his crew defended their ship, on 8th December 1941. But the Chinese were different; many Japanese thought of them as the Nazis regarded the Poles, as sub-human. In Shanghai before internment, Peggy Taylor saw Chinese being bayoneted by Japanese sentries, for minor infringements of their instructions, at the various guard posts in the city. And at the end of the war, when a crowd of young people from Yangchow went outside the camp, in a tour of the countryside, the group – Joyce Evans and Beryl Piper, Colin Palmer, Keith Martin and Mike

Ashdowne – met an elderly Chinese. He greeted them, shaking Colin's hand, and showed them

> "ghastly pictures of people on the [town] wall mutilated by the Japanese" [36]

When we consider the implacable cruelty of the Japanese treatment of Chinese, both soldiers and civilians, their attitude to us seems comparatively moderate, though obviously an individual such as Tanaka stands out because of his sadism.

---

1. For the rape of Nanking, see H. Bix: *Hirohito and the Making of Modern Japan*, pp.332-6 and pp. 340-2
2. For Hongkew, see S. D. Sturton, *From Mission Hospital to Concentration Camp*, pp.55-6 and p.62
3. H. Collar, *Captive in Shanghai* and N. Cliff, *Prisoners of the Samurai*
4. Peggy Taylor, unpublished memoir, p.7
5. Hudson Felgate, unpublished memoir, pp. 9 and 10
6. David Bolton, Walford Gillison, PRW and myself, recollections, July/August 2002
7. Beryl Piper, 9 January and 27 March 1945
8. David Bolton, recollections, July 2002 and Willis, op. cit. pp.116-7
9. PRW and David Bolton, recollections, June 2002. Also, Ian Mackinnon, recollections, April 2002
10. Eleanor Box, recollections, June 2002
11. HFW, 22 June 1945
12. Myfanwy Beynon, recollections, March 2003
13. Begley family, *Separated for Service*, p.75
14. Angus, *White Pagoda*, p.139 and HFW, 14 April 1943
15. R. Blake, Jardine Matheson, p.245
16. Elizabeth R. James, newspaper interview
17. HFW, 12 October 1944 and 23 May 1945
18. For Temple Hill, see Cliff, p.40. HFW noted Yangchow's last parade, 20 August 1945
19. HFW, 23 June 1944
20. HFW, 13 September 1943
21. Angus, *White Pagoda*, p.114

22	Mary Savage, personal account, pp.9-10, confirmed by Dennis Savage, August 2002. My own recollections follow the story as told in Willis, op. cit. p.98-9
23	Evidence of Beryl Evelyn Smith, WO 325/122
24	WO 325/122, P.R.O.
25	WO 325/122, in P.R.O.
26	Begley family, *Separated for Service*, p.78, and WO 325/122, in P.R.O.
27	Quoted in Cliff, op. cit., p.142
28	Collar, op. cit., p.138
29	Scott, G.A., *In whose hands?*, p.79
30	Cyril Mack, recollections, October 2002
31	Neil Begley, pp.115 and 136. Also Walford Gillison, recollections, June 2002
32	Beryl Piper, 13 June 1945
33	HFW, 16 March and 14 April 1943. For Yamashita at Lunghua, see Cliff, p.131
34	Keith Gillison, p.164; Keith Martin, unpublished draft memoir, p.9; Speech Day programme, Yangchow Boys' School, 24 August 1943
35	David Bolton, recollections, June 2002
36	H. Collar, cited in Cliff, p.45; Peggy Taylor, unpublished memoir, p.8; Beryl Piper, 31 August 1945

ADMINISTRATION

"The best organised of all the Civil Assembly Centres in China"

Such was the reputation enjoyed by Yangchow C. Indeed the documents which remain, most of them preserved by George Grant's daughter, indicate there was machinery to deal with everyday eventualities, and with serious crises. The Japanese position was simple; their Commandant preferred to deal with a single individual – in our case, the camp Representative, Mr. Grant. He carried a heavy burden of responsibility. But they also prescribed that we had group captains, and below them, section leaders. Their function was to arrange the daily roll-call parades, and convey information to all the ten or twelve families in each section. Apart from this the camp's administration was up to us. The Japanese supervised roll-calls, and regular patrols of the compound. Everything else was left to Mr. Grant and the elected camp committee.

The camp headquarters was situated in House No. 2, where Grant both lived and had his office. Nearby the camp secretary; at first, W. J. Brown, and latterly, Frank Parry, had his office too. Mr. Brown had issued the ration cards we all carried, entitling us to our daily food, however minute the portion. Frank Parry's signature appeared on many of the documents which survive our internment, including those to deal with such potential crises as air-raids or fire. House 2 was therefore the place where we internees resorted for any administrative matter, however small. This might be a proposal to change billets, which needed the sanction of the appropriate sub-committee, that on accommodation, before action could be taken.

As for the Group leaders, they earned the nicknames of Blockheads, since the original idea was to make each of them the leader in charge of a particular accommodation building. As far as our own family was concerned, living in House No. 1 – the former church – Owen Beynon was leader in charge of our group. The photograph taken just before the camp was broken up shows him in the middle of the group's front row, as all those belonging to the group posed in front of the church. The Blockheads' job was to arrange the daily roll-calls, indicating to the Japanese guards if any person was too sick to be present on parade. In the evenings, when roll-call took place indoors, inside each building, the Blockheads had to report that each family was present at the correct time. The documents issued by the camp administration also suggest that such group leaders should convey information to those in their groups; further they could also pass upwards the concerns which individuals might have. However, as camp routines became established, such concerns were most often directed towards one of the specialised sub-committees. Eventually there were nineteen of these, varying in size from a maximum of nine members – on the education sub-committee – to the smallest – that on the gardens which had only two members. An ingenuous feature of the system meant that one person on each sub-committee also belonged to the camp committee itself. This arrangement had the advantage that no specialised sub-committee could discuss, or reorganise matters, without continuous reference back to the camp committee proper.

Camp Committee

This was the advisory group of internees upon which Representative Grant could rely for consultation. It is clear from my father's diary that a new camp committee was chosen three times each year. Gradually, the adults in camp began to recognise those with considerable administrative skill from those who simply appeared to possess such skill. It would be invidious to mention names but it is clear that A. L. Piper, Cecil Longhurst and Ernie Hardman were universally trusted. It may simply reflect the attitude of the period, but it is strange that no woman ever served on the camp committee, though one of the larger specialised sub-committees dealt with women's affairs, and included a Belgian lady, after the Belgian contingent arrived in November 1944. Finally, my father records that on many occasions he was pressed to stand for election to this significant body. Each time he refused, believing that he served the camp as Free Church chaplain, as teacher in the school, taking his part in the regular fatigues and occupying himself with his six weekly Bible classes.

Disputes

Even in the best run institutions, disputes arise; Yangchow C was no exception. Fortunately, the machinery which existed proved adequate to deal with them. Inevitably the distribution of food was one of the most contentious issues. In the first summer of our internment, a meeting of all adult campers was summoned, to determine how the cereals and dried fruit obtained from the International Red Cross should be distributed. There were lively words as tensions surfaced between some of the Eurasians and some in the Jewish community. So heated was the debate that Mr. Grant's sympathies were torn apart by the issue. The hurt feelings aroused took some weeks to subside. [1]

Again, there was severe tension in the winter of 1944. A few campers expressed criticism of the way in which Mr Grant had behaved. Ralph Bolton, another especially trusted person as one of the camp doctors and one of the camp vice-chairmen, chaired a camp meeting which finally vindicated Grant, and awarded him a vote of confidence. Shortly afterwards, fifty campers protested against the form in which the balance sheet was presented. R. G. Morrison, who had drawn up the balance sheet, felt their criticism so strongly that he resigned, in petulant mood. It is notable that on these two occasions, difficulties occurred in the coldest part of the year, as if the weather itself brought people's grievances to a head. [2]

Mr. Willis' colourful illuminated text "Give us this day our daily bread" aroused mixed feelings in the camp community. Initially he posted it up in the dining room, with Mr. Grant's approval. But soon there was criticism of this move. A few felt the text would alienate some of the Jews, and possibly even Catholics. In Willis' own account, he tells that when the dining room was temporarily in use for a play, the text came down; this coincided with a failure in the bread supply. Feelings ran high as some people regarded the illuminated text as a mascot and believed there would be no more bread until the text was replaced. The debate continued for some weeks, until finally one of these who believed in the text's efficacy nailed it up for the duration. The bread supply never failed again. [3]

The final test came in the extreme cold of our last spring at Yangchow. Lard, made when the tiny ration of pork was cooked, was one of the few foodstuffs which we could spread on the small amount of bread which we had. A major dispute arose in mid-March 1945 over how this could be most fairly shared among us. The camp committee was offended when its proposals were received with hostility. A vote of confidence took place, with the outcome that both Mr. Grant and the whole committee resigned en masse, since they believed that the camp was behaving irresponsibly. Grant went so far as to submit his written resignation to the Commandant. But by this time, it was clear that no-one else so commanded the respect of the majority of adults. Grant was persuaded to continue, together with a committee consisting of almost entirely new members.

The machinery set up to deal with major emergencies – fires or air-raids – was highly efficient. Again the organisation by group leaders was to be used, with a team of young teenagers to act as liaison between the different groups. Their job was also to notify the camp medical personnel of any casualties who needed urgent treatment. We were fortunate that in a camp of over six hundred people there was no serious fire, nor any air-raids. Minor flare-ups in the kitchen were on too small a scale to be a serious danger. Air-raids could well have proved testing – as building or wall collapse could have meant Chinese invading the camp. This never occurred, but it was well that the organisation was put in place to deal with such emergencies, had they occurred. [4]

[1] HFW, 20 August 1943
[2] HFW, 14 and 18/19 January 1944
[3] Willis, pp. 86-9
[4] Yangchow C.A.C. Air-raid precautions, February 1945

ENTERTAINMENT

"The play's the thing"

William Shakespeare, *Hamlet*

"Let me not live … if I had not rather hear thy discourse than see a play"

Robert Burton, *Anatomy of Melancholy*, Pt.III

Such a mixed community found many ways to entertain itself, after work was done. Concerts, debates, lectures, pantomimes, music-hall, plays both sacred and secular and camp-fires – all these formed the diet enjoyed by adults, and those nearly adult. Meantime youngsters of my age were safely tucked in bed; only rarely were we allowed to stay up and join in the fun. The authorities – the camp committee and the Japanese – encouraged these pursuits, apparently believing that a busy camp was a happy camp. People today often think we internees were bored with the tedious routines of internment. Those taking part played music, acted or danced because they enjoyed it; the audiences found the result more or less diverting. At worst, an evening might be too long, or a show be feeble. If we are to believe the diaries which survive, such entertainment was normally interesting or fun. Of course, as people grew to know one another, there were parodies and verses making mock of the idiosyncrasies of those who shared their internment in Yangchow C. For instance:

"The only things she thinks of
Are water, soap and blue;
But how on earth I wonder
She washes down the stew.
The cigarettes she swaps
Appear to look so dry –"

And the subject of this? Mrs Widler, of course.

The Russians

A distinctive flavour was added to our evenings by the Russians. One of them, Mrs. Nicholls, regularly played the Rachmaninov C# minor prelude on the jangling keys of the dining-room piano; her interpretation impressed the young people, Keith Martin among them, with its tragic gloom. Later on she gave a Chopin recital and included songs in her programme. Vyvyan Dent, her accompanist for the songs, gave a brief interval talk on Chopin's work. Laura, Mrs. Nicholls' pretty daughter, delighted the audience at one of the Russian evenings with her dancing, while Olga Linkhorn sang a Russian patriotic song. Beryl Piper's opinion was:

> "A good concert, and better still, an amusing one" [1]

Another Russian lady, Mrs. Widler, was a source of entertainment in herself. She was compulsive about washing; in itself an admirable trait, but an inconvenient one at times of acute water shortage, such as we endured at Yangchow C. Her favourite refrain was:

> "I vant some vatter to vash my body."

Young Jimmie Taylor, an ornament of the Hornets' Nest men's dorm., made fun of her eccentricity in his verses. The chorus ran:

"Watery, watery, watery Widler
The Grand Sahara is calling you;
Widler, o Mysterious Widler
What wouldn't that desert swap with you.
The water's strictly rationed, Not enough to satisfy,
But the sands around Ma Widler, Don't ever seem to dry."

Camp-fires

Camp-fires were the first of the ways in which we passed the Yangchow evenings. People met at the camp-fire pole, between the church and the central well (No. 2 on the map). The group sing-songs took place after supper before the evening curfew. Everyone sat on tarpaulins and sang the old favourites: *Clementine, Old Black Joe, Home on the Range* and *Auld Lang Syne*. For accompaniment we had mouth-organs, played by Mr. Manley and a certain Mrs. Julia Tobias. The songs were interspersed with individual items. Mrs. Tobias was a star player, on a large saw; many people recall her strange instrument, perhaps because it was so idiosyncratic. Mrs. Tobias did not stay long at Yangchow; she departed for Shanghai along with those from Camps A and B. The Night Hawks, the teenage lads who had formed themselves into a band, were regular performers at camp-fire, entertaining the company with radio skits and burlesques. [2]

Peter and I were not allowed to stay up for camp-fire; however at least once during internment, a children's chorus performed at it, and both of us sang. Vyvyan Dent would finish off the evening by playing *Abide with Me* on his accordion, for people to sing.

Keith Gillison's imagination was sufficiently fertile for him to compose a new camp-fire song. It was performed by a sextet: Betty James and Gwen Morris, both my parents: Mary and Harold Wickings, the composer himself Keith Gillison, together with his wife Kath. Perhaps the song was Dr. Gillison's version of *If* – with apologies to Rudyard Kipling.

If you can queue and not be tired of queueing,
  But let the man behind you take your place –
And have some blustering fellow elbow forward
  Just turn to him a happy smiling face –

If you can do your duty in the kitchen
 And, slicing onions, never shed a tear –
And never come too late, nor leave too early –
 But quietly do your job till it is clear? [3]

Gramophone Sessions

Room 7 was the venue for evenings of gramophone music. Often these were classical recordings; Jack Kale was a lover of the classics: symphonies, concerti, and quartets by Haydn and Mozart, Dvorak and Beethoven. Beryl once attended a session of predominantly Romantic music – with some Rachmaninov, and music by Elgar and Debussy as well. Many people, including both my parents, delighted in these evenings. Owen Manley recalls the Kemp brothers, Bill and George, playing selections of their 78rpm records on a portable wind-up gramophone. They were happy to share their music with others. The sound of bamboo needles, preferred to the metal variety for their soft tone, remains in Owen's memory. A special device, shaped like a small cigar-cutter, was used to repoint the bamboo to the requisite sharpness. Edward German's *Merrie England* was played on at least one occasion, possibly in a mood of patriotic nostalgia. [4]

Lectures

With such a varied group of people it was relatively easy to find some who were ready to speak at evening lectures. The range of subjects was immense: shark fishing, piracy, the ascent of Everest. George Henderson's lecture on the 1924 assault on Mt. Everest, in which Mallory and Irvine died, was considered "brilliant and never-to-be-forgotten" by one of his audience, young Walford Gillison. We L.M.S. people had a special interest in this; was not our own Dr. Howard Somervell, of South India, one of the members of the 1924 expedition? Both Colin Palmer and Keith Martin recall my father's fascination with climbing, with the loss of Mallory and Irvine, and with the Kanchenjunga adventure, so that Keith purchased the account of

Kanchenjunga later on. One former naval officer told his tale: "Captured by Pirates". Elderly Mr. Taylor needed my father's help to compose his talk on the siege of Ladysmith in the Boer War. Some of these lectures were expository in style: Mr. Beynon spoke on X-rays, while Dr. Gell struck a sombre note with her account of lepers and leprosy. Dad too had been responsible for a leper home, during his time at Siaokan; as a small child of three, I would beg to be allowed a visit to "Daddy's leopards". Keith Gillison called his talk "Leaves from the diary of a Hankow surgeon". [5]

Of course, we lacked slides or maps: all the visual material so essential to any lecture today. Indeed, when Mr. Piper, Beryl's father, spoke on the earthquake of 1923 which devastated Japan, his illustrations caused a serious problem. Mr. Piper had drawn outline maps of the Japanese islands on a blackboard, to illustrate his experiences:

> "Suddenly a whole clankeration of guards stomped in, faces like thunder, shouting for interpreters. Ousting everyone off the front rows, they demanded to be convinced that the downfall of the Land of the Rising Sun was not being plotted by Mr. Piper, and subversive elements there present. They were satisfied eventually, and stayed till the end." [6]

Some lecturers were obviously skilled at public speaking. They made themselves heard, and varied the pace and tone of their delivery. The best of them could inject a joke, or amusing tale, into the most sombre topic, and so hold their audience's attention. Others were less experienced, so that interesting material was wasted if people could not hear properly, or if they grew restive when the lecturer spoke in a monotone.

Once we had been liberated, many of us were keen to hear about the last campaigns of the war. Captain Cox, of the U.S. Army, found an eager audience. Hudson Felgate mentions things then unknown to us: radar, jeeps and LST's - landing ships' tanks. My father noted:

> "Interesting talk on the war … Sickened by Jap. brutalities and Allies taking few prisoners, but specially by account of the atomic bomb." [7]

A few days afterwards, Col. Flowers, R.A.M.C., described conditions in western China, especially in Chungking, headquarters of Chiang Kai Shek's nationalist régime. It was depressing to hear of Chiang having a Gestapo. Next day, Col. Flowers spoke on "England and the War". So those of us planning to return to the United Kingdom will have learnt of the hardships endured by our relatives at home: bombing, V1 and V2 rockets, and food rationing.

Debates

"Tobacco: a curse or blessing to mankind"
"Spare the rod and spoil the child"

These were two of the subjects debated amongst us at Yangchow. My father was chairman for the first young people's debate. The motion was: "Classical music is more appreciated than swing"; the standard of debate was sufficiently lively for the first debate to be followed by others. Red-headed Myfanwy Beynon proposed the motion: "The present is preferable to the so-called Good Old Days". Appropriately enough, "Red" Symons seconded it. Dr. Ralph Bolton, some 20 years Myfanwy's senior, acted as leader of the opposition, with his usual wit; he was ably seconded by Betty James. Controversial topics - gambling; the love/hatred relation of the sexes – figure among the subjects chosen for debate. Who was responsible for the choice of "Money is the root of all evil" and "Are women less logical than men?" I surmise that my father will have been one of those with a hand in it, if only because he served on the adult education committee. Good speakers were found, after some effort; Beryl Piper was among those who appreciated these efforts; all the speakers in the Good Old Days debate spoke well enough to hold her attention. [8]

Variety Shows

This was the age of variety shows, when those with a taste for strutting the boards laid aside their everyday selves and adopted different personae. Eddie Weidmann did a good Maurice Chevalier act. Bud Abbott and Lou Costello were often mimicked. Music hall turns featured large in the regular Friday evening entertainments. Other stars were Barbara Manley, sister to Gilbert and Owen, Charlie McAllan – not a young man, but a girl – "Charlie" was short for "Charlotte". Dr. Riddell too, our camp dentist, was another music hall star. A large audience, including the Green and the Piper families, flocked to the first variety evening. Recitations – sometimes funny, sometimes straight – were often part of the programme: Mr. Ray, Father Thornton and Doc Ralph Bolton were among those who recited. Lively Mr. Ray invented his own radio show, which he called "Ray's Radio". Later he was to star as Widow Twanky in one of the pantomimes – *Aladdin*.

Radios were, of course, forbidden by the Japanese authorities. Consequently radio news and entertainment was one of the things we missed most, and one of the first things to be recovered at the end of the war. Two of the young men, Alec Jones and one of the Waller brothers, went into Yangchow town in search of a radio. The boys were up on the roof of the boys' dorm, fixing up a wireless aerial. Soon afterwards, people could lean out of their windows and hear music playing. [9]

Drama

"The play's the thing" - this was certainly true of us at Yangchow. Some drama was produced in a school context, but amateur dramatics had been a feature of Shanghai life, so there were plenty of people prepared to act, and others to stitch costumes, and the less glamorous jobs of assistant stage manager.

Shakespeare was favourite for school productions. In the August heat of 1943, the girls' school was rehearsing *As You Like It*; it concentrated on the Rosalind and Celia scenes, so Beryl Piper and her friends had the chance to act. Scenes from *Twelfth Night* enlivened the boys' school Speech Day in 1943: Mike Ashdowne was Sir Toby, Ted Evans Sir Andrew Aguecheek. Keith Martin wore the yellow stockings of Malvolio, while Ken Shirazee played Feste, the clown.

Following the success of *Merchant of Venice* the next year, my father adapted *Androcles and the Lion* from Bernard Shaw's original for his VIth formers. The script ran to 15 pages of close-typed foolscap. Probably this was performed for parents only. An interesting result was that "Androcles" was one of the first books Keith Martin bought after returning to England in 1945. Someone considered producing a St. Francis play, with a star part for Brother Wolf, but this idea was abandoned as unsuitable. It was not only the older students who acted: IVth form boys played scenes from Chaucer, devised by Ralph Bolton at speech day. *The Pied Piper of Hamelin* was a junior school production, during the last summer of the war. My brother Peter was narrator, wearing an uncomfortably stiff Eton collar. Apart from Leslie Green, Rosemary's young brother, as the Mayor, the rest of us were rats, of every hue, or were relegated to the crowd, as citizens of Hamelin. "Pied Piper" was meant for outdoor performance, but the unpredictable July weather was unkind. Heavy rain meant it had to be transferred to the dining-hall. According to my father, the play "reflected great credit on Beynon's training".[10]

Breach of Promise was one of the first plays at Yangchow. Mrs. Jessie Ferguson, ably seconded by Cecil Longhurst and Owen Beynon, produced it. Camp drama tended to be short, except of course for the pantomimes. Just over two years later, my parents went to see a well-acted murder play, *Ten Minute Alibi*.[11]

Pantomimes

One of the episodes in a pantomime set the camp talking:

> "Do you remember Bubsie? She came to the notice of our crowd overnight when she appeared as a harem dancer in one of our camp pantomimes – dressed in a diaphanous net costume. All our eyes popped, and from then on several besotted youths trailed and sniffed after her."

This is how Owen Manley described the deep impression made on him by the hula hula dancing of Fay Westwood, nicknamed "Bubsie". Reactions to her dancing were mixed. Someone with show business experience commented on Fay's talent, telling her to consider taking up dancing as a profession. The more Puritan element found the hula too suggestive: one or two of them condemned it as disgusting. [12]

Aladdin, the most memorable of the Yangchow pantomimes, was performed on three successive days in April 1945. This long-heralded production starred Geoff Baker as the Genie, Mr. Ray as Widow Twanky, and young Peter Gibson as slave of the lamp. Peter had to chant:

"Rub-a-dub-dub, Ah, there's the rub
You must know where to rub it!"

My father apparently turned down the offer of a prominent part in *Aladdin*. Someone must have been impressed with his acting in the school staff concert, in *The Spanish Tragedy*, together with Betty James and Ernie Hardman. All three of them had laughed their way through rehearsals just before Christmas 1944. Judging by the cast list, *Aladdin* was obviously a big affair. The determination of producers and cast to put on the show is impressive when we consider the severe cold of January and February 1945, and the paucity of electric light, which must have made rehearsals very difficult. "Super". So young Rosemary Green thought it; she was obviously impressed for she went to all three performances. [13]

Dances

The dining-room became a dance-hall each Saturday evening. The authorities allowed the dancing to continue after the 9 p.m. roll-call, which was checked by the block-heads in each of the houses. The dancers could enjoy themselves up to 10 p.m. Beryl Piper, on half-term leave from school, and so temporarily one of a baking team, went to the Bakery Ball, a particularly grand occasion. Normally those under 17 were considered too young for the Saturday frolics. They were forbidden to dance by Mr. Tait, though sometimes they watched the older ones.

Younger teenagers could go to their own "kids' dance" – as Beryl refers to it. These were separate occasions, held mid-week. Sometimes special features were included: a waltz competition, for instance. Sadly one such competition became a farce, when most youngsters were too scared to compete. Beryl wrote afterwards:

> "Boy was I mad! Kenny, the fool, and I, and one other couple were the only participants ... I told Kenny off, but he was sorry". [14]

The week following, some older ones wanted to join the kids' dance. There was a row, as Mr. Tait tried to exclude some of the over-17's, despite protests from young men like "Red" Symons, "Buzzy" Wade and Denis Savage. Two of the older girls, Joyce Evans and Van Beynon, wanted to join in, too. [15]

Even in the middle of internment, young people could dream. Indeed one could argue that fantasy about the future – fantasy of repatriation, meeting loved ones again, dreams of freedom, sustained us through the long months in camp. Possibly the Saturday night dancing inspired

Beryl's dream. It consisted of a shopping expedition, in which she bought a brown hat, silk stockings and high heels to match. To complete this "snappy outfit" her final purchase was "a cute brown fur coat". In a restaurant nearby, she met a young chap who ordered four slices of chocolate cake and an ice-cream soda for her. Her "nice dream" was rounded off by the music playing throughout. Certainly we all dreamt of food: people leafed through old magazines, savouring the luscious meals therein. "Reading home recipes makes one long for cheese and cake" wrote my father, soon after we reached Yangchow. As for Beryl, it may be that the new clothes and high heels were at least as important at the time as the luxury food. People's imaginations were obsessed with food, but to a girl in her late teens, a snappy outfit was, maybe, even more significant. [16]

Dance music was sometimes live, when Mrs. Mulvey tinkled the ivories in Victor Sylvester mood. More often the gramophone supplied music. There was always a last waltz; in this closed society, whose lifeblood was gossip, it mattered a great deal who danced the last dreamy number with whom. Waltzing was popular. For Empire Day 1944 Marjorie Train, Geoff Baker, Jean McLorn and Charlie Scharnhorst, tall and dark, were dancing. Marjorie's long full white skirt was set off by its red and blue sash; the skirt was one of her mother's tablecloths in real life. Marjorie had borrowed a record of the *Blue Danube*, so as to practise her waltz steps, some days before. When the 10 p.m. curfew arrived, all the young people agreed the evening was far too short. [17]

Concerts

"We're Going Home"

1. No more queuing for Yangchow stew,
    No more sharing a room with you!
    No more hunting elusive bugs,
    No more itchi and no more k'u
    No more roll-call and whistle too
    For there's no place like Home

Chorus   We're going home! We're going home!
　　　　　We're on the road that leads to home
　　　　　We've had enough of living rough,
　　　　　and now we want the real stuff
　　　　　at home, sweet home

2.　　　No more stokers, nor labour squad
　　　　No more pleasing six hundred odd …
　　　　No more sitting on wobbly chairs
　　　　No more yelling for shoe repairs …
　　　　No more saving up rags for mops
　　　　No more dodging the fierce camp cops
　　　　For there's no place like Home

Chorus

3.　　　No more tofu and no more yams
　　　　No tombolas for Canteen jams
　　　　No more ointments supplied in shells
　　　　No more fishing for tins in wells
　　　　No more millions of C.R.B.
　　　　No more blocks for the militree …
　　　　For there's no place like Home

Chorus

　　　　　"Colin's mother gave a piano recital – so elegant in her
　　　　　long gown – I loved the evening – out-of-this-world
　　　　　treat" [18]

Colin's mother was Mrs. Lillian Palmer, Colin Palmer then being in the VIth form of Yangchow school, hoping for a career in medicine. Some of our concerts were single-person recitals, like this.   Mrs. Anna

Nicholls, as we have already seen, was another solo performer. But more often there were more performers, often with recitations interspersed between musical items. Songs like *We're Going Home* were our promise to ourselves that somewhere, beyond the stone walls and Japanese patrols, the bugs and the roll-calls were the familiar things of 'home'. The words of *We're Going Home* reflect the irksome features of internment, trying to salvage humour and decency from the slide into degradation and despair. At the words "No more sharing a room with you!" the chorus line on the stage would shout, and stab their fingers at people they knew in the audience. As for the "wobbly chairs" in the second verse, no camp function could be held, unless people brought their own chairs, whether upright ones, or more frequently, those of the canvas folding variety. And tombolas were used in our camp, as in other CAC's, to share out goods in short supply, whether jam or other goodies.

Besides *We're Going Home* there were other ditties; *D'ye ken Yang Chow, with its ...* was one of these sung, of course, to the tune of *D'you ken John Peel*. Who composed these verses? It is difficult now, nearly sixty years later, to discover who was their author. One of the camp "poets" was Jimmie Taylor; he wrote the verses about Mrs. Widler, and a long poem about the Hornets' Nest – the young men's dorm.

Jimmie was an odd person who strutted around the camp, something of a figure of fun to the teenagers of the community. He was no beauty spot – his ruddy complexion was scarred with acne, and he wore thick-lensed spectacles. Jimmie was 27 by the time the war was over. His father had kept a philatelist's shop in Shanghai, prior to internment. Both his parents were also in camp – Mr. & Mrs. W. J. Taylor – but Jimmie lived apart from them. Perhaps the fact that he suffered from epilepsy made him something of a loner; if so his lone wolf status allowed him the time to compose these light verses: some of the emotional glue which now binds us Yangchow folks together.[19]

Camp life was by no means all fun and frolic. All these forms of entertainment were cooked up after most people had done a day's work, whether in the bakery, as part of the Public Works Department, or at school, as teacher or student. Often the difficulties were considerable, whether they were owing to severe weather – rain drumming on the roof, when someone was attempting to give a lecture – or to practicalities such as lack of electric light. Nonetheless the show went on. Survivors recall the nasty, and often non-existent, food of Yangchow but we also recall our star parts, whether as a Shakespearean figure – the Merchant of Venice himself, or the noble Duke – or even as a humble rat from the streets of Hamelin town.

---

[1] Beryl Piper, 21 January 1944
[2] For Mr. Tobias, see Walford Gillison and Peter Gibson, recollections, September 2002; Beryl Piper 17, 18 and 20 March, also 19 May 1943.
[3] HFW, 9 June 1943
[4] Beryl Piper, 21 February 1944; HFW passim; Owen Manley, recollections, October 2002
[5] HFW, passim
[6] Owen Manley, recollections, October 2002. Also HFW, 13 September 1943
[7] Hudson Felgate, unpublished memoir, p.12 and HFW 4 September 1945
[8] Beryl Piper, 12 April 1943, HFW passim
[9] Beryl Piper, 28 and 30 August 1945
[10] Beryl Piper, 9 August 1943; boys' school Speech Day programme, 24 August 1943. HFW, 15 August 1944. Keith Martin, recollections, March 2003. HFW, 28 July 1945.
[11] HFW, 29 June 1945
[12] Owen Manley, recollections, September 2002; Angus, *White Pagoda*, pp.136-7
[13] Peter Gibson, recollections, September 2002; HFW, 4 and 8 December 1944, also 19 April 1945; Rosemary Green 19, 20 and 21 April 1945.
[14] Beryl Piper, 11 January 1944
[15] Beryl Piper, 18 January 1944
[16] Beryl Piper, 19 February 1944 and HFW, 26 March 1943
[17] Beryl Piper, 24 May 1944
[18] Myfanwy Beynon, recollections, March 2003
[19] Keith Martin, recollections, November 2002

FESTIVITIES

Christmas

True to British tradition we tried to make something of the two Christmases we spent at Yangchow. We had real Christmas cheer, carols, children's parties, and a surprising number of small gifts were exchanged. In 1944, our family had a celebration tea with Gwen Morris, then in hospital, and later on, games with Gwen's friend, Betty James. We children had a great day.

The Christmas fare in 1943 was stewed duck, a tremendous treat, savoured the more because it was not Same Old Stew. Apparently the Japanese secured a sizeable share for themselves. By 1944, the camp cooks had acquired both guile and skill. The authorities agreed when asked if we could save up our meat ration for two weeks before Christmas. The sumptuous dinner was pork, sweet potatoes, carrots and gravy, all cooked separately, rather than the usual coagulated mush. [1]

In both years the camp rang with carols; the Catholics joined with other Christians to practise them in 1944. And both years there was a nativity play. In 1943 this was simply a tableau, with fair-haired, blue-eyed Marjorie Train as a striking Madonna. Two girls, coached by Mrs. Newman, spoke the prologues: Zena Goodman and Beryl Piper. After this success, the producers were more ambitious at Christmas 1944. Most participants had spoken parts; the Virgin Mary had to learn the entire Magnificat. More could go wrong; a number of mishaps occurred and hardworking Mrs. Begley was reduced to tears as angels' haloes fell off, or a nervous actor forgot his lines. Nonetheless it looked superb, framed by Mrs. Manley's long velvet curtains; claret in colour, they were used for all our stage productions. [2]

New Year

The first New Year's Eve, a special party was held in Room 7; all the young people were there, including Father Thornton. Salmon pie, a treat made from the tinned salmon included in our parcels, was on the menu. Then there was dancing with Stirrat Miller and Charlie McAllan among the revellers, until it was time to see in the New Year.

"Goodbye, Old Year, you've not been so bad; I've grown up a lot in 1943" wrote Beryl Piper. She was right; all those in their late teens and early twenties had to mature, as they worked alongside the adults, and took their turn at the tedious chores of camp life. [3]

Festivities were on a grander scale in 1944. People could imagine an end to internment. The war was obviously going our way, and greetings were exchanged in hopeful mood. With powdered noses, and carefully preserved jewellery the girls prinked, and found their prettiest frocks; they found the dining-room bright with decorations made from coloured handkerchiefs. People brought their bedspreads to wriggle their way through the conga. Sonny Nissim and Eddie Weidmann starred in the floor-show. Matti Nissim enticed a few of the girls to try some booze, probably rice-wine smuggled in possibly by the glamour-girls, or the coolies who removed the coal-ash. After all the kissing and greeting, the young people wandered around the grounds in the fine moonlit night. [4]

---

[1] Willis, p.102 and Beryl Piper, 25 December 1944
[2] HFW, 7 November 1944; Beryl Piper, 25 December 1943 and 1944; Marjorie Train, recollections, June 2002, and Owen Manley, recollections, October 2002
[3] Beryl Piper, 31 December 1943
[4] Beryl Piper, 31 December 1944

SPORTS AND PASTIMES

"in games confederate" [1]

Football, softball, hockey: people played these regularly at Yangchow. The former mission compound had plenty of space for playing-fields. A few internees came equipped to organise these sports.

Owen Beynon, the lively Welsh pharmacist, directed the energies of the young lads, with enthusiasm. Football was the boys' first love. My brother vividly recalls his first goal, a moment of triumph.

"Fluke!" yelled the others: the ball ricocheted from his knee, looping straight between the posts. These remained from the time when the compound was an American mission.

They also played a form of touch rugby, learning to tackle, to swerve and score tries. Beynon as coach taught them the rules, and the mysteries of offside. David Bolton, small then for his age played scrum-half, while Peter, my brother, captained the youngsters' team to a victory of 18-17 points. Cardiff University rugby songs in Welsh were memorable.

> "'Y' Varsity Ygorrah!"

echoes still in David Bolton's mind. [2]

Beynon's short square figure, clad in shorts, whistle around his neck, ran to and fro on the touchline, with the eagerness of a friendly terrier. It may be that his enthusiasm was the greater as he had no son of his own. "Zest teaches"; this was supremely true of Owen Beynon. Parents were grateful to him for his commitment to the lads, teaching them how to work as a team, and how to bear their knocks with fortitude. None of the boys who came under his influence forgot O.G.B.

Hockey was often an after-school sport. Beryl Piper was outstanding. She scored all four goals for her side, captained by Audrey Begley, which won 4-1 in the second of two matches. Her friend Marjorie Train was on the same side, Joyce (Evans) and Van (Myfanwy Beynon) among their opponents. Hockey was an all-girls activity, as football and rugby were restricted to boys, unlike softball. [3]

Softball – the American version of rounders – was all the rage with the young people. The season began in mid-March, when Mr. Beynon threw the first ball in the match the School and the Rest. Team names were usually far more imaginative: a bevy of girls formed the Mermaids who took on the Ancient Mariners. The Mermaids sported white shirts and shorts; Beryl Piper – the main authority on this, played, along with Marjorie Train, Ella Sequeira, Joyce Evans, and Nora Quincey – the only Yangchow bride. The great variety of bird life gave their names to the Sparrows v. the Blue Jays, the Mynahs v. the Orioles.

Father Thornton, the young Jesuit, was a star, putting all his lank energy into the game. He played as a youthful exception to the Ancient Mariners, as did Mr. Willis, Father O'Collins. Young players included the Wades, Nissim, "Bully" Bulldeath, and Phillips. [4]

Cricket was a minority sport. Shortage of the requisite bats, bails, stumps and gloves was a problem. So too was costume. David Bolton and Walford could never both play cricket: there was but one pair of white shorts to fit. Sharing was impossible; obviously a handicap to aspiring Test cricketers. Maybe finding 22 chaps eager to play was another difficulty. [5]

Boys were organised for early morning gymnastics, by Peanut Quincey; he had had a gymnasium in Shanghai. His physical training meant exercises to develop muscles in the limbs and stomach. Neil Begley remembers using bricks instead of weights. The lads became surprisingly fit after hundreds of pushups and situps. [6]

Boxing was an all-age activity. Matches were played in sequence, with the smallest and lightest lads first, and continuing through to the heavyweights. Among the most appreciative spectators were Japanese guards. Filling the front rows, the guards evidently regarded themselves as patrons. As more and more blood was spilt, their happiness increased. In their turn, they exhibited their own martial arts, after one specially bloody boxing bout. Boxers who won secured an extra loaf of bread as a prize; half went to the loser, by secret prior arrangement. Walford's father, Keith, encouraged his son to box, despite his own non-violent beliefs. [7]

All these were organised sports; teams and results were displayed on the camp notice-board. But children's best games are always those played without adult intervention. Marbles were a constant source of delight. We played on the bare ground, digging holes and trenches in the dust.

"Look at my big blue monster marble! It's all swirly – and look it's bigger than yours!"

"No, it ain't … Besides, I've got more than you! And that's right, 'cos I'm older."

"So what? I always beat you – twice yesterday, and three times the day before!"

Of course we traded them, or lost favourite marbles to superior players. Peter, my big brother, always had more marbles than I, and better ones, at that.

We girls played sissy games, like house, with our dolls. But, with more enterprise, our gang laid tracking routes around the camp. Brownie activities gave us the idea; our gang Moira, Sheila Macdonald, Joan and I made the game our own. Two girls laid the trail, tracing arrows in the dust, with plenty of false trails and dead ends to confuse the following pair.

In the cool of evening, we played kick the can or hide and seek, using the plentiful shrubs and trees as hiding-places. The boys knew all the trees because of the birds' nests they contained. The boys rose early, to rob the golden orioles, doves and cuckoos of their eggs. Their own ethic ruled no-one took more than a single egg but the number of lads stealing an egg each from the same nest was unlimited. The eggs were blown for the collections of Colin Henderson and Neil Begley, the leading collectors. Brenda Henderson, Colin's widow, keeps Colin's collection of birds' feathers, with a diagram showing the sites of the nests they plundered. The camp committee's ban on egg-collecting merely spurred on the lads. In the hour before dawn, Peter Jewell and Albert Nissim stole out, but Albert fell, losing his grip on a damp branch. Afterwards he found it

> "punishment enough to be laid up in bed for three weeks" [8]

Best of all, we delighted in playing in the watery pools which lay under the trees after a violent thunderstorm. Fierce drops of rain hit the ground; there was the fine fresh smell of deliverance from the thunder, and lightning. After the downpour, pools of water – twenty or thirty feet across – formed under the sycamores. Out we went to gather up the cicada shells found among the leaves. These too we gathered, to serve as boats for our cicada passengers.

Cicadas were the big brown grasshoppers; they made a shrill chirring sound through the summer heat. Boys and girls alike competed to have the largest collection. David Bolton tried to convince the Wolf Club authorities that 100 cicada shells qualified him for the collectors' badge. He failed, miserably.

Grownups forbade us to wade in the water; they threatened us with nameless diseases if we disobeyed. The temptation to cast aside our battered sandals and roll up our ragged garments, was too great. We pushed the leaf-boats across the bays and inlets of the biggest pool. The supreme moment came when you could tip your rival's cicada from its leaf. I longed for a stream, to dam, and paddle in.

"Where go the boats?" Stevenson's poem with its echoes of far-off places and distant lands seized my imagination. The camp was a safe haven for us youngsters; we could not escape, but we played undisturbed by the rumours of war, which cast so deep a shadow on the lives of our parents.

We quarrelled of course: older ones bullied and tyrannized over younger ones. Big ones showed off, even if it was only their huge black stag-beetles, with awesome pincers, kept in a matchbox. Older girls, jealous of my academic prowess, warned of the ghastly effect that nibbling bright green elm-leaves would have on my stomach:

"That Dr. Gillison! He'll have to cut you open, see if he don't." At six, I was young enough, and credulous enough to believe their tales.

Life was a strange blend of China: its trees, flowers, birds, hot, hot sunshine and sharp showers, and England. Parents talked of 'home' – grandparents, aunts and uncles; they showed photos. But England was faraway – too remote to be worthy of consideration. Dr. Bolton used to say

> "Churchill says that … but I [David Bolton] had no idea who this was, or what he was talking about." [9]

Camp life was queuing for food, roll-call, school, Cubs and Brownies – living outside under the trees in the summer; in winter, shivering inside, tucked into the warmest garments our parents could find.

Empire Day, May 24th

Who now remembers Empire Day? Yet we observed it, in all three years. Children's Day was the name given to it by the camp authorities, in an attempt to trick the Japanese into the idea that May 24th was just another sports day. Soon they realised its true name:

"You no longer have an empire!" jibed the guards.

The afternoon included all kinds of races: relays, hopping races as well as the usual 440, and 880 yards race. Throwing the cricket-ball and a massive tug-of-war. There were prizes! Even if they were recycled gifts from fellow-campers, they seemed splendid enough to the winning children. Adults won soap, cigarettes, matches and sugar – all luxury items by camp standards.

1945 was a special Empire Day. It was clear by then that Japan was on the defensive. "WE" were going to win; it was only a matter of time. The occasion was specially marked with a maypole dance, and open-air drama, scenes from England, Scotland, Ireland, Wales, and from the dominions – Australia, Canada and South Africa.

"Fair"

was my father's terse comment; "imperialism" was a dirty word to him. [10]

---

[1] Wordsworth, *The Prelude*, Book I, l.414
[2] David Bolton, recollections, June 2002, and HFW 23 November 1943
[3] Beryl Piper, 10 February 1944
[4] Beryl Piper's diary, passion, and Willis, p.73
[5] David Bolton and Walford Gillison, recollections, June 2002
[6] Neil Begley, *An Australian's childhood in China*, p.107
[7] Walford Gillison, recollections, June 2002
[8] Neil Begley, p.103 and Albert Nissim, recollections, December 2002
[9] My own recollections, and those of David Bolton, June 2002
[10] Beryl Piper and HFW, entries for 24 May in 1943, 1944 and 1945

THE END

Parachutes and peaches

Parachutes drifted down from the sky, dropped from huge American bombers; silken umbrellas of rainbow colours: red, turquoise, grass-green, white and gold. They had a double significance: first, that we were not forgotten. Our need for food and clothing, cigarettes and medical supplies had been recognised by the world outside. But also the wonderful nylon fabric was useful. It was a marvellous novelty, for all sorts of purposes, at a time when our supply of fabrics was low, and most textiles had been used two or even three times already.

That first drop, on 5th September 1945, was not very successful, in practical terms, since so many of the packages dropped by the planes landed far outside the confines of the camp. Young men, and older ones too, had to rush outside, and stake their claim to the oil drums containing the valuable food and clothing. My father was only one of many who went well beyond the North city wall. He stood by till younger men and teenage lads reached him. Between them they carried the goods into camp. These planes from Saipan did not seem to have learned much from the solitary plane which had flown over four days previously, in a reconnaissance flight. Indeed so wild was the drop that a considerable amount of damage was done to Chinese property, with many house roofs smashed in. Mr. Grant appointed my father to investigate Chinese claims for damages to their property. This made the last four weeks in camp a very busy time for him. [1]

The most dramatic episode of the parachute drop was the hitting of one of the camp buildings. A vast 100-gallon drum smashed through the roof of one of the tallest buildings, descending rapidly through all three of its storeys, to the ground floor. Fortunately the two people in one of the rooms through which the oil drum passed were standing close to the window. They would have been killed if they had been sitting on the bed. Frances Henderson and Kath Gillison only just escaped severe injury, as the oil drum crashed through. Later on a second drop of a different kind was made; a parachute brought a supply of plaster of Paris, for the broken leg of Mrs. Flo Solomon. [2]

Finally, we must not imagine that all the foodstuffs arrived intact. In the first drop, more than one of the metal containers burst open with the force of its impact. This cracked the casings of some tinned peaches so that the juicy fruit spilled on to the ground. So hungry, and so deprived of fruit were some of the boys, that they scooped up the peaches directly from the ground, using only their fingers to convey the food to their mouths. [3]

Of course, the camp medical authorities warned us that too much food could be dangerous, especially when we had been on such short rations for six months and more. Most people took heed of this advice and added the American goodies in moderation. Others disregarded it, and suffered as a result, by over-eating the powdered milk, Spam and chocolate which their stomachs could not easily digest.

Liberators

At this confused and tense time, just after the Allied victory, we had strict instructions to stay inside the camp. This was difficult for the adventurous, who were eager to explore. Nonetheless the order was that no-one was to go outside, unless he had the express permission of Mr. Grant, or of his deputy, A. L. Piper – father to Beryl. A few shopping expeditions into Yangchow were allowed; Jean Willis went, to buy sewing materials, but even then she and her companions were escorted by a Japanese guard. [4]

Our American liberators who arrived on 3rd September made a strong impression of glamour. Captain Cox (U.S. Army) together with five other young officers were bronzed and handsome in their uniforms. We children stared: they seemed like Greek gods. The young ladies, of course, found their most attractive garments, and tried to distract the officers from their real job: to wind up the camp, and evacuate us all to Shanghai as soon as possible. The saddest event of this time was the death of Geoff Manley. On the brink of manhood, his death was attributed to a violent form of dysentery; possible despair at the prospect of an uncertain future sapped his will to live, or so some of his friends believed.

Only a few days after the Americans, a British contingent also reached us. Captain Martin, easily recognised by his red beret, was in charge. The excellent relations between both sets of liberators made for easy co-operation in the task of terminating the camp.

By now the previous camp routines had been broken. Chinese youngsters from nearby schools visited us, to congratulate us on the Allied victory. They brought sweetmeats of many kinds with them: purple-pink bars of sugary substance symbolised joy. To our immense regret Peter and I were forbidden to eat them. Neither were we allowed to attend the evening celebration dinner. This grand occasion in which 60 internees met the local Chinese leaders – guerrillas and civil officials – was marked by speech after speech. My father regretted his fluent Mandarin when he found he had to translate them as the three-hour banquet continued on its way. [5]

One of Captain Martin's best ideas was to organise a series of picnics, for all age-groups in turn, in the countryside beyond the city. For many whose experience of China was confined to Shanghai, this will have been a novelty. For all of us the picnics were memorable, as we savoured the freedom we had missed for so long. Our own family joined the picnic in late September when we visited the water-girt areas north west of Yangchow city, and crossed the elegant Lotus Lily bridge near a temple, before our return to camp. Another novelty was to hear first the Americans and then British officers describe the later developments of the war, especially radar, new-style landing craft and details of the campaigns in Europe, Italy or Burma. There were formal lectures – sometimes overloaded with technical terms. Many of us found simple conversations as absorbing as the lectures proper.

Departure

Now people started to leave for Shanghai, first in groups of fourteen or fifteen, then in larger ones of twenty-five to thirty people. Among the first to go was Mr. Grant, so long looked up to as our leader. His experience in administering Shanghai's wharves and harbours made his presence there a priority. Mr. Piper remained in charge, until we all finally left, by the first week of October 1945. Mr. Savage, the victim of Tanaka – in the infamous bath-house incident where the Japanese was so cruel – had already been to Shanghai, where he learned that the Allied authorities' orders were to wind up the camp immediately. Our family was among the last to leave, as Captain Martin hurried to and fro, and people recognised that they would have to leave a few belongings; it was clear Chinese guerrillas would swarm over the walls once we were gone, to salvage anything they could find. We travelled by barge to Chinkiang down the Canal; then we were transferred to the station and marshalled into groups of four, to find space in the crowded railway carriages. Tired, in need of a wash, I fell asleep on my father's shoulder as the train steamed towards Shanghai. As his diary recorded:

> "Not a bit like a Sunday ... "[6]

---

[1] Peter Jewell wrote up the details of the U.S. supply drop, after research into the U.S.A.F. archive, in the post-war period.
[2] Gillison, p.166
[3] Mary Lou Newman, recollections, June 2003
[4] Beryl Piper, 10 September 1945
[5] HFW, 11 September 1945
[6] HFW, 7 October 1945

APPENDIX I

CAMP RESIDENTS

William Abel; Miss Maureen Abel; Fred Abel; Miss E. Anderson; K. Ashdowne; M. Ashdowne; Hilary C. Ashdowne; Michael Ashdowne; Harold Atkinson; Mrs. Nimi Atkinson; Walter R. Atkinson; Mrs. Flora Azachee; Miss Ray Azachee; Raymond Azachee; Joseph Azachee; Miss Aziea Azachee.

Violet Baker; Geoff C. Baker; Roony Baker; E. S. A. Barraclough; Mrs M. J. Barra; Mrs. J. M. C. Baynes; Maj. Colin Begley; Audrey Begley; Edith Begley; Ian Begley; Neil Begley; Mrs. B. Bennett; Owen G. R. Beynon; Mrs. A. Beynon; Myfanwy Beynon; Joan Beynon; Dr. Ralph Bolton; Eileen Bolton; Tom Bolton; David Bolton; Miss Mollie Bolton; James Bowie; Susan Bowie; Ella Bowie; Margaret Bowie; W. G. Bown; Mrs. N. Bown; Miss Evelyn Bown; Norman G. Bown; W. J. Brown; Clara M. Brown; Miss H. A. Brown; H. W. Brown; Mrs. R. F. Brown; Miss G. Brown; Miss Brenda Brown; G. R. Browne; Mrs. Elena Browne; Robert Bulldeath; Miss Winifred Bunn; Mrs. A. F. Burke.

J. M. H. Clark; Mrs. G. A. Clark; Miss Virginia Clark; R. Cook; Mrs. Lilee Cook; Mrs. D. E. Cook; Mrs. M. Corneck; A. H. Crank.

Gordon J. Day; Mrs. M. D. Day; Christopher Day; Elizabeth Day; R. V. Dent; Mrs. E. Dent; A. D. Denton; Mrs. L. Denton; David Denton; Mrs. M. W. Dickson, Jean Dickson; Margaret Dickson; E. R. Duckitt; Mrs. M. Duckitt; Rosalie Duckitt.

Joseph Evans; Mrs. A. L. Evans; Edward (Teddy) Evans; Miss Joyce Evans.

Reginald Hudson Felgate; Mrs. W. G. Felgate; Miss Reginette Felgate; Reginald H. Felgate (II); Mrs Jessie Ferguson; Hugh Finnigan; Mrs. M. Finnigan; Hugh Finnigan; P. J. Fisher; Mrs. J. Fisher; Mrs. J. Foox; Miss D. Foster; W. E. Fowler; Mrs. C. M. Fowler; Gloria Fowler; Mrs. C. V. Fraser; Miss Heather Fraser; Miss Sonia Fraser; Stuart Fraser.

A. Garin; Miss M. Garin; Mrs. M. Gater; Miss G. Gater; Dr. Mary Gell; H. L. Gibson; Mrs. M. Gibson; R. Kenneth Gibson; Peter L. Gibson; Dr. Keith Gillison; Mrs. Kathleen Gillison; Walford Gillison; J. S. Gittens; Mrs. S. Gittens; Jimmy Gittens; H. Gilmer; Alec Glass; Moira Glass; O. A. Goldenburg; T. G. Goodman; Mrs. M. Goodman; Miss Z. Goodman; John Goodman; J. E. Gordon; J. H. Gordon; J. E. Gordon (Jr.); J. F. Goodman; George Donald Grant; J. E. Gray; Mrs. W. L. Gray; Miss Yolande Gray; G. G. Green; Mrs. F. K. Green; Miss Rosemary Green; Leslie Green.

R. C. Hall; Mrs. J. C. Hall; Ernest Hardman; Mrs. M. F. Hardman; J. Hart; Mrs. K. S. Hart; W. Hay; Mrs. A. Hay; Miss Emma Hay; N. Hayward; Mrs. S. Hayward; M. Hayward; Miss R. Hayward; Miss Hebe Hayward; Miss R. Hayward; Jack Hayward; Ronald Headington; Mrs. Phyllis Hayward; Miss C. H. Hayward; Rev. George Henderson; Mrs. Frances Henderson; Colin Henderson; A. Hillaly; Mrs. S. Hillaly; Miss Mercia Hillaly; Miss J. H. Hillaly; Miss Estelle Hillaly; Miss J. H. Hillaly; Miss Hilda Holms; Miss Victoria Holms.

Mrs. M. Irvine; Miss Jean Irvine.

Miss Alice Jagger; Miss Elizabeth R. James; Miss E. B. Jameson; Mrs. M. B. Jameson; Miss G. Jefferis; P. J. Jennings; Mrs. Gertrude Jewell; Peter M. Jewell; Mrs. E. R. Judah; Mrs. Manya Judah; Miss Valerie Judah; Cyril R. Judah; Miss Gloria Judah.

Jack R. Kale; Mrs. G. K. Kale; John Kearns; Mrs. A. Kearns; Miss M. Kearns; Terence Kearns; Charles Keenan; Mrs. L. K. Keenan; Miss Augustine Keenan; George Kemp; Mrs. Sophie Kemp; William (Bill) Kemp; Miss Edyth Kemp; Dr. Chadwick Kew; Mrs. Florence Kew; Ernest Kew; Allen Kew; Lionel Kew; W. H. Kimberley; Mrs. A. K. Kimberley; Miss Era Kimberley; Anatol Kosloff; Miss Kirene Kosloff; Miss E. Kosloff.

H. R. V. Lamb; Mrs. Olga Lamb; Harold Lamb; Thomas Lamb; Ronald Laycock; Mrs. Katherine Laycock; Willie Lee; Miss Marjorie Lee; Miss Mabel Lee; Mrs. R. Levy; Miss Seemah Levy; William Lewis; Mrs. Tamara Lewis; A. N. Lewis Mrs. K. N. Lewis; Miss Katherine Lewis; Mrs. Olga Linkhorn; Michael Linkhorn; Mrs. M. Litter, Miss Vera Liter; Cecil Longhurst; Mrs. S. Edwina Longhurst; Miss Patsy Longhurst.

Mrs. A. Macdonald; Miss J. Macdonald; A. C. Mack; Mrs. D. Mack; Mrs. M. G. Mack; Miss Millicent Mack; Robert G. Mack; Cyril Mack; Ian Mackinnon; Miss M. Mackintosh; N. Mackintosh; Frederick Madar; Mrs. M. Madar; Miss Joyce Madar; Miss Gloria Madar; Miss A. Madar; G. Madar; G. A. Madar; Miss Crecia Madar; Miss D. Madar; Miss Effie Madar; Allan F Madar; Sydney Main; Mrs. C. Main; Miss Marjorie Main; Miss Joan Main; Richard Malone (Silent); Miss Maud Malone; Miss Agnes Malone; William T. Manley; Mrs. Frances Manley; Richard Manley (Ric); Geoffrey Manley; George N. Manley; Mrs. Yvonne Manley; Miss Barbara Manley; Owen Manley; Gilbert H. Manley; P. W. Mansfield; Mrs. F. Mansfield; Mrs. C. Mansfield; Mrs. A. Marco; N. J. Marr; Mrs. J. V. Marshall; Miss Edna Marshall; Keith J. Martin; June M. Martin; Rev.

Philip C. Mathews; Mrs. M. McAllan; Miss Mary McAllan; Miss C. B. McAllan; Miss Joan McAllan; W. A. McDonald; Mrs. M. S. McDonald; Miss Mary McDonald; Miss Sheila McDonald; A. M. McGregor; Mrs. I. McGregor; Miss Ella McGregor; Capt. William McIlwain; Mrs. H. McIlwain; Miss M. McIlwain; Mrs., J. McLorn; Miss J. McMurray; Mrs. E. Mende; Mrs. N. Mende; J. Miller; Mrs. H. S. Miller; Miss Muriel Miller; Stirrit Miller; Walter A. Millward; S. J. Moalem; Mrs. G. Moalem; Joey Moalem; Miss Lily Mogra; Miss Molly Moline; Miss Winnie Mooney; Miss Gwen A. Morris; R. G. Morrison; Miss Maida Morton-Smith; L. Moses; Mrs. F. Moses; A. E. Moses; Cyril Moses; Miss A. Moyhing; Miss E. Moyhing; Eddie Moyhing; C. P. Mulvey; Mrs. E. M. Mulvey; F. D. Mulvey; J. Munro; Mrs. F. Munro; Mrs. M. Myerscough.

R. D. Neville; Mrs. A. L. Neville; Miss A. Neville; Mrs. P. L. Newman; Miss Mary-Lou Neville; Mrs. A. Nicholls; Miss E. Nicholls; Reggie C. Nicholls; Mrs. T. V. Nicholls; Miss Loretta E. Nicholls; Saul G. Nissim; Mrs. Flora Nissim; Miss N. Nissim; Miss R. Nissim; N. M. Nissim; Matook R. Nissim (Matty); Salem R. Nissim (Sammy); N. F. Nissim; Matthew Albert Nissim; Miss Rachel Nissim; Miss (Ra)Mona Nissim; William C. Norman; Mrs. S. Norman; Miss Ann Norman.

Father Michael O'Collins; H. A. Ozorio; Mrs. D. H. Ozorio.

Walter A. L. Palmer; Mrs. Lillian Palmer; Colin A. L. Palmer; Frank Parry; Mrs. C. E. Parry; Miss Carol Parry; Miss Aileen Parsons; F. G. Penfold; Mrs. A. A. Penfold; Miss Joan Penfold; Gus Pereira; A. G. Pereira; M. A. Pereira; Mrs. L. A. Pereira; Miss Irene Phillips; Terence E. Phillips; T. Phillips; Reggie C. Phillips; Mrs. H. (Nell) Picozzi; A. L. Piper; Mrs. G. L. Piper; Beryl Piper; G. H. Popple; Mrs. M. H. Popple; Leslie Popple.

C. E. Quelch; C. W. Quelch; John G. Quelch; Lewis P. Quincey; Mrs. P. I. Quincey; Miss Leonora Quincey.

G. D. Raeburn; Mrs. E. Raeburn; Miss Elizabeth Raeburn; Peter D. Raeburn; M. V. de Rago; C. E. de Rago; C. M. de Rago; Miss P. M. de Rago; F. S. Ramplin; Mrs. F. Ramplin; Miss Doreen Ramplin; Miss A. L. Ray; Herbert Ray; M. B. Ray; I. R. Razon; Mrs. N. Razon; Richard Razon; George Read; Mrs. M. R. Read; Miss Joan Read; Alf Read; Mrs. E. R. L. Read; G. Tony Read; Mrs. Daisy Rees; Miss Gwen Richards; Dr. Jimmy Riddell; Mrs. Dorothy Riddell; Mrs. G. Roach, Joan Roach; J. R. Roche; Mrs. M. E. Roche; Miss E. Z. Roche; A. A. (Gussy) Roche; H. B. Roe; Mrs. A. M. Roe; David E. Roe; H. Rogers, V. Rose; Mrs. G. Liddy Rose; Eddie G. Ross; Miss Grace Ross; Mrs. M. S. Rudland; B. Rudland.

T. Sands, Mrs. N. Sands; Gordon F. Savage; Mrs. G. Savage; Miss Mary Savage; F. J. T. Savage; Denis F. L. Savage; J. S. Schuker; Mrs. H. Schuker; Miss S. J. Schuker; Miss T. J. Schuker; Sydney Schuker; Stanley Schuker; Jack R. Schuker; Mrs. L. N. Scott; Miss L. D. Scott; A. A. Sequeira; Mrs. M. M. Sequeira; Miss Ella Sequeira; Norbert (Sonny) Sequeira; C. B. Scharnhorst; Mrs. R. Scharnhorst; Miss Milly Scharnhorst; Mrs. H. Sharrock; Miss E. Sharrock; Miss Eleanora Sharrock; S. G. Shaw; Mrs. Winnie Shaw; E. A. Shaw; Miss Hilda Shepherd; Miss E. K. M. Sherrif; B. A. Shirazee; Mrs. D. M. Shirazee; Kenny Shirazee; E. C. Shirazee; Joe da Silva; Mrs. M. C. da Silva; Robert da Silva; Miss M. Silver; Miss Ann Silver; J. L. Simmons; Mrs. C. A. Smith; Mrs. Doris A. Smith; Miss Amy Smith; Miss Stella Smith; Mrs. S. E. Smith; Miss F. C. Smith (Jimmy); S. J. Smith; Mrs. E. A. Smith; Miss Beryl E. Smith; Brian D. Smith; Brenda M. Smith; Miss E. Smoleff; M. B. Smoleff; Mrs. L. Solomon; A. S. A. Solomon; Mrs. H. Solomon; Miss Flo Solomon; Miss Juliet Solomon; Miss R. Solomon; Miss S. Solomon; Miss S. Solomon; William H. Spencer; Mrs. Z. I. Spencer; Billy Spencer (W. H. Jr.); R. K. Stott; Mrs. Patricia Stott; Mrs. M. L. Stuart-Murray; Miss A. M. Stuart-Murray; A. T. Stubbs; Mrs. E. L. Stubbs; Mrs. A.

Stubbs; Mrs. C. Sullivan; Dr. Rob G. Symons; Mrs. A. Symons; Miss Florence Symons; P. Symons; Donald C. Symons (Red); W. Symons; Miss Ann Symons.

Alex Tait; Mrs. L. F. Tait; Miss M. E. Tait; Miss Helen Tait; Mrs. E. Tangier-Smith; Mrs. C. A. Tatlock; Jimmie Taylor, Mrs. Ruby Taylor; Miss Peggy Taylor; Miss M. C. Taylor; W. H. Taylor; Mrs. E. H. Taylor; W. J. Taylor; Mrs. L. Taylor; John T. Taylor; Miss Margaret Taylor; Robert Taylor; Mrs. L. Taylor; Colin O. Taylor (baby born in camp); C. W. Tebbutt; Mrs. C. J. Tebbutt; Miss Edyth Tebbutt; Miss C. H. Tebbutt; Charlie Thompson; Mrs. M. V. Thompson; Miss Beaty Thompson; Geoffrey C. Thompson; Rev. James E. Thornton; Miss Cary Todd; Miss J. R. Toeg; P. Tomlin; Mrs. M. T. Tomlin; Miss P. C. Tomlin; Jimmy Tomlin; C. E. Tomlin; Mrs. H. Tonkin; William H. Train; Mrs. Jean T. Train; Miss Marjorie Train; Mrs. A. M. Travers; Mrs. M. Tresize; David Tresize; E. N. Trueman; Mrs. P. E. Trueman; Gus Tully; E. W. Turnbull; Miss Barbara Turnbull; Mrs. S. Turnbull.

Mrs. S. Underwood; Jack R. Underwood; Miss Chris Underwood.

Mrs. Mary Vier; Miss Joan Vier.

J. L. Wade; Mrs. F. M. Wade; Lionel J. Wade; Lancelot T. Wade (Buzzy); Miss Edith Wagstaff; Frank Walker; Mrs. D. Walker; F. H. Waller; Mrs. E. L. Waller; Lewis Waller (Slim); E. A. Waller; Edgar J. Waller; W. Jimmy Ward; R. W. Ward; Mrs. L. Ward; Miss Laurel Ward; Mrs. M. Ward; Miss C. Ward; Eddie Weidman; Mrs. R. Weidman; R. Wescombe; Mrs. G. Wescombe; Mrs. A. Westwood; Miss Fay Westwood; Miss Alice Wheal; Mrs. A. White; Miss Agnes White; Miss J. Wickers; Miss O. Wickers; Rev. H. F. Wickings; Mrs. M. D. L. Wickings; Peter R. Wickings; M. Grace Wickings; Mrs. N. Widler; Miss Ethel Widler; E. S.

A. Williams; Mrs. M. F. F. Williams; S. J. Williams; Mrs. M. S. Willis; G. Chris Willis; Mrs. Jean O. Willis; Miss Helen Willis; John A. Willis; Mrs. Elizabeth Willis; Miss Nora Willis; Sir Cyril Young; Lady G. Young; Miss Margaret Young; Michael C. H. Young.

Belgians: arrived 16 November 1944

Mrs. M. Badour; G. Badour; C. Barbe; Mrs. M. Barbe; J. Barbe; J. Barbe; F. Barbe; A. Brusselmain; Mrs. S. Brusselmain; A. Delabis; Mrs. G. Delabis; A. Delabis; H. L. Demesse; Mrs. L. Demesse; Miss G. Demesse; P. Donay; G. Donay; C. Gavels; N. Ley; Mrs. G. Ley; F. Mertons; Mrs. S. Mertons; Miss L. Mertons; A. Noltinck; Mrs. S. Noltinck; F. Peater; C. Piron; E. P. Tercalaures; Mrs. L. Tercalaures; Miss J. Tercalaures; H. L. Tercalaures; Mrs. A. Tercalaures; Miss J. Tercalaures; L. Vanderhelst; F. Verhaest; Mrs. A. Verhaest; P. Vissers.

APPENDIX II

BIBLIOGRAPHY: PUBLISHED WORKS

Angus, Fay (née Westwood)	The White Pagoda, 1978
Ballard, J. G.	Empire of the Sun, 1994
Begley, C. Neil	An Australian's childhood in China under the Japanese, 1995
Begley family	Separated for service: a biography of Colin Keith Begley and Edith Mary Begley, 1994
Bell, F.	Undercover university, 1991
Bix, Herbert	Hirohito and the making of modern Japan, 2000
Blake, Robert	Jardine Matheson: Traders of the Far East, 1999
Cliff, N. H.	Prisoners of the Samurai, 1998
Edwards, Jack (in collaboration with Jimmy Walter)	Banzai, you bastards!, 1991
Gale, Geoffrey L.	Interned in China, 1946
Gilkey, Langdon	Shantung Compound, 1966
Gillison, Keith	The Cross and the Dragon, 1988
McAll, Frances and Kenneth	The Moon looks down, 1987
Main, Joan	Diary – in Imperial War Museum
Mason, W. Wynne	Prisoners of War, 1954
Power, Desmond	Little Foreign Devil, 1996
Scott, George A.	In whose hands?, 1946
Stead sisters	Stone, paper, scissors, 1991
Sturton, Stephen D.	From Mission Hospital to Concentration Camp, 1948

Titherington, Arthur   Kinkaseki, 2000
Velden, Doetje van   De Japanse interneringskampen
                            vor burgers gedurende de
                            tweede, 1963

Wang, George and Barr, Betty   Shanghai boy, Shanghai girl, 2002
Wasserstein, Bernard   Secret War in Shanghai, 1998
Waterford, Van   Prisoners of the Japanese in
                            World War II, 1994

Willis, G. Christopher   I was among the captives, 1947

BIBLIOGRAPHY: UNPUBLISHED MATERIAL

Diaries of:

    Zena Goodman   )
    Rosemary Green   )   all interned in Yangchow C
    Beryl Piper   )
    Harold Frederick Wickings)

Unpublished memoirs of:

    Hudson Felgate   )
    Joan Main   )   all interned in Yangchow C
    Keith Martin   )
    Peggy Taylor   )

Public Record Office

    WO 325/122

Imperial War Museum

        Misc. 73 (1105) : Memorabilia relating to Beryl Evelyn Smith

The School Fifth Form – with H.F. Wickings the author's father, Rev P.C. Matthews, headmaster, and Miss Joan Penfold, headmistress in the centre.

Yangchow Years

House Number 1 – The residents of the church. Author on extreme right, front row.